PRODUCED FOR THE FESTIVAL OF INDIA

Editor ASHARANI MATHUR

Assistant Editor SONYA SINGH

Designer GOPI GAJWANI

Phototypeset at Children's Book Trust, New Delhi

Specially published on behalf
of the Festival of India by:
Brijbasi Printers Pvt. Ltd.
E 46/11, Okhla Industrial Area,
Phase II, New Delhi-110020.

First Edition published 1988.

ISBN NO: 81-7107-010-8

BRIJBASI

India

Specially published for the Festival of India

Message

India and Japan are countries whose achievements have left a mark on the world. Both of us have long histories. Both of us have a great future. It is important that we should know each other better and work together closer.

There are, fortunately, old links between us. Buddhism paved the way for exchange of scholars, artists and pilgrims. In more recent times Japan's industrial progress has evoked great interest in India. There is vast scope for cooperation, technological as well as cultural.

It is good, therefore, that our two countries decided to organise reciprocal Festivals. The Festival of Japan in India was widely popular. It enabled our people to have a glimpse of the arts which Japan has nurtured with such loving care.

The Festival of India in Japan is aimed at providing the people of Japan an insight into the rich cultural and philosophical heritage of India, celebrated for its depth, diversity and persistence. We hope that it will carry a special message of friendship and peace, of tolerance and compassion.

I give my good wishes to the Government and people of Japan.

New Delhi
February 25, 1988

RAJIV GANDHI
Prime Minister of India

Contents

The tree in India, myth and symbol

LAKSHMI LAL

A banyan tree in the heart of India.

The trees of India stand tall in the sap of centuries. It flows rich and full in their veins as symbol, myth and legend. The wisdom and the folly, the sense, the nonsense and the commonsense that is India show as much in her tree-lore as in her great systems of philosophy or metaphysics. For India lives at many levels.

In India, more than anywhere else, the tree is much more than just a tree. It bears a load of symbols and the weight of an ancient religious tradition that was born and bred in her many forests. The Indian way of penetrating to the heart of any matter has always been through the symbol. India is a great seeker, as she is a great storyteller. The search is all. The symbol, and whatever tale happens to hang thereby, is a proven instrument in that search. Hence the welter of myth. Again, the symbol is closely linked with the Indian concept of *maya*, the veil of illusion. Is a spade really a spade? Softening a hard fact into a symbol—a resilient, absorbent and plastic medium for truth—is one of India's great talents. It also serves as a concomitant to the question of existence as *maya*.

As a consequence, the Indian mind shifts from fact to illusion to reality to truth, adeptly side-stepping life's pitfalls and journeying through to its destined end. And all the while we keep a tight hold on reality—and the symbol. The Indian literally "senses" an object till it begins to stand for more than itself and becomes a morsel of experience, a symbol, in fact.

Once perceived, the symbol leads past itself through layers of meaning to fresh insights. And if this process is a collective, continuing, racial habit of mind, we have symbols that grow and link into feasible systems of life and thought. As they have in India. A way out of the *maya* of it all. For it is through 'symbolic' cogitation that the Indian has hit upon yet another common Indian activity— transcendence. A symbol, by definition, transcends the concrete. And there is little denying that life is largely a matter of confronting and then transcending the so-called concrete realities. Much of Indian escapism, I make bold to say, is nothing but transcendence.

And now we come to one of our most enduring and beloved symbols, the tree. It grows through the myth and legend of India, taking root in the Indian consciousness, shading its great visions, guarding its buried treasures of thought and feeling. A tropical profusion of ideas cling to this symbol—superstition, magic, necromancy, speculation, wild flights of fancy and imagination, hidden fears, horrors, joy, sorrow, contentment, enlightenment, sheer poetry—for it has been a long and eventful time in the making.

To begin at the beginning is to begin with the forest—

Above left : "Yakshi under a tree" sculpture in red sandstone,.2nd-3rd century A.D. Courtesy Department of Cultural Affairs, Government of Punjab. Above right : "The Vision of Markandeya", Pahari miniature painting, 18th century A.D. Depiction of a creation myth from Matsya Purana. *Courtesy Chandigarh Museum. Opposite page : Maya clasps the sala tree in this bronze depicting the birth of the Buddha, Nalanda, early 9th century A.D. Courtesy National Museum, New Delhi.*

the natural habitat of the tree. Many of our guidelines for living, our speculations, enlightened or otherwise, have come out of forest workshops and seminars on Truth which led to the great texts of the *Brahmanas*, the *Aranyakas*, the *Upanishads*. Much of our teaching was done in forests by sages who ran exclusive schools away from the distractions of town and city or even home. The first of the four stages of life, *brahmacharya*, the intensive learning stage, was ideally passed in a hermitage. The third and fourth stages, retirement (*vanaprastha*) and withdrawal (*sanyasa*) also took one to the forest. The forest then, was almost an institution, a formalised training ground for life, here and hereafter. It was a veritable school for symbols.

Our epics celebrate forest life even when it is a part of exile, as in the epic *Ramayana*. Chitrakoota and Panchavati, the forest homes of the exiled Prince Rama and his wife Sita, symbolize conjugal bliss, the *parnakuti* (leaf-hut) being the ideal home of the ideal couple. Associations lead to symbols. The *Puranas* talk of recreating a panchavati in one's private garden with the planting of five (*pancha*) trees—the peepul, the banyan, the *bilva*, the *amalaka* and the *ashoka*. This is how the Indian lives out his symbols.

The forest is a living, pulsing presence. In the epic *Ramayana*, the first encounter the god-prince Rama has with evil is through the female demon, Tataka. Her mere presence had laid waste large tracts; the evil in her had sucked the life out of her environment. Then Rama arrives, she is killed and the forest comes alive in a burst of smiling relief and blossom. Happiness, Valmiki seems to say, is a forest in flower and, of course, the forest was never just a forest. The personification and the symbolism are vivid and unmistakable. Again, Sugriva describing his brother Vali's prowess to Rama, trembling at the very thought, recounts how Vali had only to stride past for the mighty *sala* trees to shed their leaves in fright. Man and Nature

Above : small shrine under a peepul tree. Above right : the banyan majestically spreads its aerial roots.

interacted with an intimacy that spoke of a close and bonded relationship.

From forest to grove, park, garden and avenue was natural progression. The taming of wild nature into more companionable forms gave rise to fresh symbols. Planting and conservation became acts of duty and charity enjoined by the *shastras* (law books). Rite and ritual took over. According to the texts of the *Agni Purana*, a conservation rite becomes a soul-saving act and the trees themselves objects of veneration, appeasement and invocation. There is also a detailed description of a model garden, giving positions of specific trees and shrubs and an adjoining flower garden. A household garden, true, but explicitly ritual in concept. The forest had been brought home and familiarity was turning trees and plants into presences with human demands, useful presences at that. They were

beginning to wear their symbols with an air of noble ease. Close proximity, perhaps, magnified their needs in the eye of the beholder.

Trees now began to acquire a personality, an aura and an area of power and influence, and inevitably, divine patronage. Temples had *sthalavrikshas*, trees connected with their installation. Trees were being draped, in other words, with increasing symbolic significance.

And here the legends and mythology begin. Pressed between the pages of history and prehistory, our trees speak of a sylvan past, peopled by spirits, demons and deities as they frolic, sport and preside over votive or festive rites. Mallinatha, commenting on a verse in Kalidasa's *Malavikagnimitra*, lists ten trees and their longings while waiting to burst into bloom. Each one demands a different cajolement from a young and beautiful woman before it

Above : girls swing on trees during the Teej festival.
Opposite page : sculpted serpent stones enshrined at the foot of a tree.

gives birth, that is, flowers. The *priyangu* craves a touch, the *bakula* thirsts for a mouthful of wine, the *ashoka* a kick, the *tilaka* a glance, the *kurabaka* an embrace. The *mandara* longs for soft speech, the *champa* for a sweet provocative smile. The mango wishes to be blown upon, the *nameru* favours song and the *karnikara*, dance. The general symbolism is clear—youth, beauty, love, awakening, fertilisation, fecundity. But the caring individuation speaks of intimacy and a deep-seated conviction that Man and Nature stem from one source; one elemental, undifferentiated substance.

The myths of creation, of which there are many, pinpoint the place of trees in nature's hierarchy. According to the *Bhagavata Purana*, the trees are the first among Brahma-Prajapati's creations. In another version, in the *Shatapatha Brahmana*, the Creator having created Agni, fire, feared for his own life. He rubbed his palms together and produced butter as an offering, saying "Drink, as you burn." It was this rite that produced trees, plants and herbs. In both myths, trees acquire symbolic significance. In the first, they assume chronological pride of place, and in the second, they are an answer to the Creator's prayer, no less! The tree is beginning to acquire an august lineage with divine connections.

There are two motifs that the tree in India is inextricably linked with—water and the serpent. In a creation myth in *Matsya Purana*, the wandering, ageless sage, Markandeya, comes upon an infant on a banyan leaf, then a boy under a banyan tree in a vast sea. The child is the Primeval Being, Narayana, Purusha (Man) who rests on the waters of being on the coiled serpent Sesha (residual), stuff of life. An early Buddhist legend about the Buddha's enlightenment has the same symbol syndrome. In a dramatic account, ten thousand worlds resounded with thunder when he saw the light. He sat for seven days under a peepul, then moved on for another seven days to a banyan, and lastly to the tree of the Serpent King. In the moist recesses of its roots lived the cobra king Muchalinda, who sheltered the Buddha from a raging storm with his outspread hood. When Buddha emerged from his trance, Muchalinda stood, hands folded in worship, transformed into a gentle youth, ready to receive instruction.

Another mystic episode establishes the tree-serpent-water linkage. Balarama, elder brother and companion-incarnation with Krishna, was considered to be actually an incarnation of Sesha. His end comes as he sits lost in thought on the seashore at Dwaraka. A serpent crawls out of his mouth and into the ocean—his real self rejoins the formless abyss, the waters of life.

In Karnataka, sculpted serpent-stones (*nagakals*) are left, immersed for six months in water by the image-maker—a symbolic entry of water as the life-giving element: they are then set up under a peepul or a banyan for regular worship. In Kerala, sacred groves called *Kavus* are set apart for snakes. The practice supposedly started from Parashurama, an incarnation of Vishnu and legendary founder of Kerala. It was a measure intended to keep the inhabited areas clear of snakes for the original settlers.

From representing an undifferentiated, informing force, trees began to stand for separate powers—spirits, demons, deities. The forests of Buddhist legend are full of chatty tree spirits, *yakshas* and *yakshis*, busily managing the lives of their fellow beings. In Vedic and in Upanishadic times, priests and sages transmuted their forest experiences into symbol—ritualistic at first, and later, speculative. The bank of symbols was growing.

An account of just two of our major tree symbols makes

a gripping chronicle of times and places past, modes of thought and feeling now merely vestigial. Yet they are reminders of a living symbolic presence on many ceremonial occasions today, house-warming ceremonies, marriages, festivals, funerals. For the Vedic chant, *shruti* ("that which is heard"), and other forms of the oral tradition, still prevail. The Indian way of life inescapably binds you down to its myth and legend.

The first among trees is the *aswattha*, the Bo Tree, or the peepul. There is no way of challenging or disputing this. The Buddha saw the light under it. The god Krishna, in the sublime Hindu text of the *Bhagavad Gita*, speaks of it in no uncertain terms. First, in Chapter 10, in the midst of a torrential flow of stunning metaphors that establish his lineage and cosmic stature, he refers to himself as the "*aswattha* among trees". In an equally unforgettable series of five verses in Chapter 15, he designates the peepul as the cosmic Tree of Life. It spreads beyond sight and knowledge, both above and below, baffling in its mystic inversion, with roots above and branches below. Only the axe of detachment can cut through to the roots of this mystery of mysteries. In these verses, symbols are hoisted on to every part of the peepul by the Lord, the leaves are the *Vedas*, and so on, till the whole of Creation and Causation sits firmly perched on it, ensconced forever. It is an elaborate metaphor and coming from the Cosmic Hero himself, not to be taken lightly.

The *aswattha* or the peepul as master-symbol attracts scores of associations. Jyeshtha, elder sister of Lakshmi and bringer of bad luck, resides in the peepul; hence it is only to be touched on Saturdays when Lakshmi comes visiting her, it is recommended. Else, bad luck dogs you. Vaishnavi, female energy of Vishnu, one of the Saptamatrikas (seven mothers) sits under it. It features as an object of worship on a Mohenjo-Daro seal. In the *Atharva Veda*, the peepul is used in a rite to ensure a male child. The peepul is an aggressive, virile, male image—naturally, since it is symbolic of the Cosmic Purusha (Man). It is used, therefore, in battle rites where its fierce, destructive, hostile powers are evoked. The *aswattha* grows into other trees, uniting, penetrating, destroying. One can see both the sexual and the conquering elements that are associated with this tree of trees. In the *Chandogya Upanishad*, it is the focus of the sun's rays and therefore, of knowledge, light and time—the sun being the source of all these. It is believed to shower *soma*—the joy, the abundance, the elixir of life, the nectar of the gods. The heavenly *aswattha* has *soma* growing under it.

The *aswattha* is indeed the prime Indian tree-symbol. In comparison, the fabled *kalpataru*, Indra's wish-fulfilling tree, seems a jewelled artifice. Every village has a peepul as the centre of its social and religious activities. The Indian consciousness has invested it with values that open secret doors and lay bare the treasures of Indian thought. It is a tree that takes this heavy load with the graceful forbearance of an enlightened soul, the Indian goal and ideal. No concept seems too large or abstract and equally, no idea or fancy or even whim, too small or trite for it to receive. That in itself symbolises a basic Indian attitude, acceptance—very often mistakenly construed as resignation. To receive is to absorb, to grow. It is a positive act, as productive as the peepul, strong support of Indian life.

Coming a close second in importance is the ubiquitous banyan. Its aura is one of majesty and extent. Its aerial roots are its own regenerative as well as destructive force, as it spreads and acquires fresh territory. It stands for death not as finality but as renewal in the on-going cosmic process. In the *Matsya Purana* myth it bore the Primal

Being as the prophetic babe on its leaf, floating on the waters of life. The *Chandogya Upanishad* gives it the authority of privileged speculation. In a famous dialogue between Svetaketu, the avid student and his wise teacher-father, Svetaketu is asked to bring a banyan fruit. "Split it," said the father, and then—"what do you see?" "Miniscule seeds," replied Svetaketu. "Break a seed," instructed his father, ordering a second scrutiny. "I see nothing," reported the son. "That, which you do not see, is the *sat*, the essence," declared the father. "The whole huge tree grew out of that *sat*. You are that, Svetaketu."

The banyan has its deities too. Aiyanar is one of our

Trees of a Himalayan forest.

Above : the delicacy of spring blossoms in this exquisite Pahari miniature painting "Waiting for Krishna", 18th century A.D. Courtesy Bharat Kala Bhawan, Varanasi. Opposite page : symbols of life and hope—trees in a desert.

more esoteric gods. He is, in parts of south India, the guardian deity of the village and sits under the banyan tree. Dakshinamurthi, the aspect of god Siva as teacher, communicates the truth silently to his pupils, seated under the banyan tree of knowledge. It was under a banyan that Satyavan died and his wife Savitri began her famed argument with death, at the end of which she emerged triumphant and won her husband his life.

There are too many trees and too many stories to even list here, but mention must be made of the *sala* and the *ashoka*. The Buddha was born as his mother, Maya Devi, stood holding the branch of a flowering *sala* tree in the Lumbini grove. And she dreamt of his coming under an *ashoka*. The *ashoka* has associations both secular and sacred. It is one of the five flower arrows of Madana, the god of love. Vasantha (spring), his inseparable companion, appears dressed in *ashoka* leaves. Sita sat out her prison term in Lanka in an *ashoka* grove: and the tree flowers only when kicked by a beautiful woman. The symbolism is remarkably consistent—spring, love, beauty, women and fertility. The *ashoka* blooms as an enduring symbol of rejuvenation.

Myth and symbol twine round our trees like flowering creepers and the stories spread their fragrance down the years. The emotions evoked by these cover the whole spectrum of human experience—and the symbol survives. The grove remains the Indian ideal of peace, the forest a spiritual refuge. Eroded soil and values or denuded forests cannot wholly diminish the strength of this abiding symbol.

Architecture and Indian identity

GAUTAM BHATIA

Indian architecture is like a view into a forest. Obscured by the profusion, at first the eye sees only dense vegetation in a state of confusion, conflict and chaos; it is only when the focus narrows to a single tree, a shrub, a blade of grass, that the forest's variety is discernible, and an order emerges. A gaze into Indian architecture would create a similar illusion. The overwhelming wealth of buildings that form the streetscape in any Indian town, or the myriad low-key forms of its numerous villages, at first only confuse. They are forms, buildings, silent reminders of the turbulence of empire, or the humble efforts of rural craftsmen, or the selfconscious accretions of a modern housing area. They may be at once awesome and complex, as intensely archaic and anachronistic as they are appropriate and sophisticated.

They are Indian, the healthy accumulations of a varied history, the products of a single culture—and indeed the most significant record of its continuity.

The Indian city in the contemporary architectural set-

Above : Fatehpur Sikri in the early morning : a series of connected public and private spaces. Right : window of mud hut in Banni decorated from the outside.

ting promotes the inevitable comparisons between the old and the new, between the selfconsciously monumental and the naively human, betwen massive fortresses of rock and ephemeral houses of mud. But the village in India lives in a state of benign impermanence. The numbers are too many and their spread too distant to come under the corrupting influence of modernism. They have to this day remained largely unaffected by the demands of a growing industrial tradition. And in their separateness they have evolved their own variations, relying less on changing tastes and new designs, conforming instead to the ancient dictates of land, resources and climate.

In India it would be untrue to say that one Himalayan village is an accurate representation of all mountain settlements. The Indian landscape is itself remarkably varied and has produced its own localized forms of architecture. While the heavy stone and slate constructions of the Kumaon Hills protect the inhabitant from the cold, the equally heavy mud structures of Bikaner offer its residents similar protection from the scorching desert heat. The craftsmen building and domesticating these varied landscapes have, over generations, come to recognize the forces that shape them. Over the years they have carefully observed the sun and the horizon, local experience and phenomena. Along the coast or on the mountain, in the dusty plain or in the desert, the home builder understood the elements and their associations, and comprehended the nature of the materials available.

Slowly a process of intuitive building gave him a hold on the land, and the buildings and settlements he has generated from this understanding are supremely appropriate to his terrain. He has learned to live with it rather than in it. The mason and craftsman building these houses have evolved a local vocabulary of construction. Over the years they have even managed to devise surprisingly sound innovations.

The remote villages of the desert, of Banni in Kutch,

Above and top right : two views of the palace complex at Padmanabhapuram showing the strong unifying factor of the indigenous building tradition.

Opposite page : street scape in Jaisalmer showing the narrow alley ways and the overhanging buildings. Above : intricately carved screens and balconies allowed the woman of the house to gaze at the streets below—detail from a haveli, Jaisalmer.

western India, in particular, exhibit similarly evolved attitudes to habitation. Separations of caste and class necessitate that members of the same community live together. Houses are therefore grouped in a cluster formation; intuitive knowledge and local material dictate that the houses be made of circular mud walls, spanned by a conical roof of bamboo and thatch; and finally the hot and dry climate requires that the building be closed to the sun but open to air. Windows cut deep into the mud wall to ventilate the interior; they occur logically at ground level, where the family sits while inside.

Though many of these rural constructions may be structurally unimpressive, and by their very nature may not command the most dramatic sites, they express very succinctly the values of a culture and the collective and shared intelligence of a people. Their instinctive command of local materials is something no architect can equal. A gentle organic architecture, it is close to the ground from which it has risen, and closer still to the lives that have created it.

This organic concept of architecture as part of people's lives is inherent in the Indian tradition. Form and function were a seamless whole; the *sthapati*, the nearest equivalent to the architect, was the master of space, whose spatial organization created enclosures for different functions. Wood and stone were carefully worked by skilled craftsmen, whose role in traditional Indian architecture was very important. The sensitive and intelligent response of Indian builders to changing needs and circumstances allowed the built form to evolve, to acquire graceful accretions, to absorb and assimilate influences from outside and re-state these in the local idiom. This adaptability and versatility gave us an amazing heritage of cities and secular buildings through the centuries. Mud huts, palaces, pleasure pavilions or city homes: they are visually different yet the instincts that have shaped them are the same.

Instinct also wrote the script for the varying streetscapes of traditional Indian towns. Surrounded by protective walls, many medieval settlements created their own introverted architecture. The street was always narrow. But its narrowness had a positive aspect, for it opened in a series of controlled "accidents" onto public squares, open, airy; the result not of a public ordinance but of co-operation among neighbours, or at times, the natural outcome of a desire to save a tree.

A dense collective form of settlement always relied on contrast and juxtaposition to induce spatial variety into its fabric. The street was forever changing, creating moods in its own natural rhythm, accelerating movement by its narrowness, producing repose and meeting by its openness.

The surrounding architecture producing streetscapes was itself made of common mass-produced elements. Balconies, window-frames, doors and water spouts were the common ingredients of building, and each house-owner was entitled to build as he wished, assembling these in his own peculiar way, according to his own particular needs. The craftsmen making these elements knew nothing of how their handiwork would be assembled and it was precisely in their ignorance that the architecture achieved its uniqueness.

Behind the facade, the privacy of home called upon the builder to personalize and invent; but always within the strict confines of an architectural frame. A sandstone structure of small rooms, tightly arranged around a court-yard, gave the house the essential shape of a rectangular box, closed from the sides but open to the sky. This

became the fundamental form; its variations were numerous. It is in the stone *havelis* or merchant homes of Jaisalmer that such architecture has reached a profound sophistication.

The medieval city of Jaisalmer is in the heart of the desert of Rajasthan. Scorching heat, sand storms and desert breezes are some of the climatic factors that have shaped the city and its life. The narrow winding alley ways are cool and shady, the overhanging buildings on either side providing relief from the sun. The streets broaden into *chowks* or squares, open areas which are community meeting places and locations of shrines and wells.

The city of Jaisalmer is densely packed, with thousands of homes or *havelis* built close to each other. Rising on arched base and heavy plinths, the facades of these homes reach up across irridescent stone screens, dissolving the parapets into the sky. Inside, the larger openings of the rooms look inward upon the internal, indeed eternal, courtyard. It is here that the members of the house converged and met as a family, before retreating to their own spaces in the stone walls. The functions of this private courtyard were many. It allowed in light and air, it was where children played, a washing area. Activity that could not be contained in the adjoining rooms spilled over into the courtyard, a meeting place within the home, just as the *chowk* was the meeting place outside.

Details, too, marked a degree of refinement rarely achieved in domestic architecture. Every change, every movement was acknowledged and meticulously articulated in the design. Prominent thresholds marked the entrance to each room; storage closets were worked into the face of the wall; and windows recessed into alcoves became tiny rooms in their own right, receiving the light from outside and diffusing it into the larger room of which they were a part. The wall of the upper rooms had balconies and carved screens so that breezes could flow in. The intricately carved screens, as fine as lace, were not only a decorative elements, but allowed the women of the home to gaze through at the streets below. Such architecture was always un-selfconscious. Born of necessity, its refinements over seasons and generations of builders evolved a singularly powerful vocabulary of elements: the court as the outdoor enclosure, the screen wall as the element making the enclosure, and the pavilion as a place of repose and quiet. All these elements had variations in size, materials and assemblies and thus produced the variety in architecture, and yet because they were common to all buildings they gave a sense of unity and distinction to street and city. For a building in a hot climate this was indeed a sensible system of structuring.

Such elements were to consistently appear throughout history, but they were modified to suit the particular requirements of the building, its location and intent.

In the larger complexes like Fatehpur Sikri, built by the Mughal emperor Akbar in 1571 A.D. as his capital, these changes and adaptations were subtly modulated into a formal expression. The court, the pavilion, the *jali* or pierced screen were used; but they became exaggerated to express the monumental and imperial intent of their builder, Akbar. Islamic rulers asserted their greatness through their palaces and citadels, burial places and ceremonial gateways. Yet the buildings at Fatehpur Sikri do not just suggest a monarch's megalomania. True, a certain grandness was necessary in planning and executing as gigantic an enterprise as a city, but Akbar was never one for convention. Breaking away from the axial aspects of Islamic planning, the palace precinct emerged in a series

of staggered courts, enclosed by sandstone arcades and walls, and conforming to the dictates of the rocky terrain. The uniqueness of this complex, however, was not in its deviations from symmetry but in the facility of its architect to reconcile the monumental and the intimate, and to intelligently manipulate the court, the wall and the pavilion so as to create the desired effect in space. In the Diwan-e-Am, the Court of Public Audiences, for instance, building elements were deliberately overscaled in order to reflect the coming together of large numbers of people, while the Diwan-e-Khas or the Hall of Private Audience next to it was made of components reduced to reflect the intimacy and closeness of the encounter. The architecture was conceived to reflect the public and private realms of building, with intimate spaces giving way to those of an appropriate public monumentality, each offering different experiences of scale and volume.

Similar concerns were also effectively expressed in buildings of other regions where the building styles were completely different. An example is the Padmanabhapuram Palace, once the residence of the royal family of Travancore, situated in south India adjoining the state of Kerala. At Padmanabhapuram, the elements took on a refinement rarely matched in the architecture of the north, a refinement not only of building technique but of space as well. As in Fatehpur Sikri, the differentiation of function dictated that the private residential quarters of the royal family receive the seclusion of the upper floors under the steep pitch of the Kerala roof, a framed wood structure controlling the light and the quality of air. The darker passages below housed the service and storage areas; while the ground floor took on a degree of openness suggestive of meeting and public interaction. A series of bridged connections between buildings united this lower floor into a precise network of circulation which brought together the diverse halls for music performance, dance, and public council.

Wood was used as liberally as stone was at Sikri. It

Opposite page : circular houses grouped in a cluster in Banni, western India.
Top : detail from a roof construction, Banni, western India.
Above : modern construction in mud designed by young contemporary architects Vasant and Revathi Kamath. Note the similarity to the Banni cluster.

Wood, liberally used at Padmanabhapuram, was assembled through an elaborate system of joinery.

formed the supporting framework of column, bracket and roof, only secondarily serving as an infilling of intricate screens, bridges and staircases. It is obvious that the master craftsman here was the carpenter and not the mason. Not only did the wooden members perform the function of support, they were assembled through an elaborate system of joinery, the rafters notching into beams, the beams cut into the column. Padmanabhapuram Palace remains an unparalleled example of superb architecture in wood. The flooring—a combination of shell lime, charcoal and other local materials—has a black and glossy finish, enhancing the serenity and repose of the whole complex. Finally, what sets the palace apart from others of its kind is that it was not conceived as a single grand gesture, the whim of a despotic ruler, but grew slowly, over a period of four centuries, building by building, adapting to the changing circumstances of time and thereby always remaining a part of the present. Despite the interesting mixture of styles in the later building what gives the whole complex its cohesiveness is the strong unifying factor of the indigenous building tradition. Though this tradition may have been influenced by the wooden structures of the Far East, it translated these alien techniques into a wholly Indian vocabulary using local materials.

But Indian architecture has always been one of assimilation, mutation and adaptation. The great waves of migration throughout history brought their own brand of building, a type alien to India. But, as always, the strengths of India's own traditions, its powerfully affecting climate, changed it, contorted, shrunk or expanded it, and made it part of its own. It was only in complexes like Sikri and Padmanabhapuram that the concentrated lessons of Indian craft, the complexity of the spaces they generated, came into a comprehensible focus. And it is these very projects—conceived, executed and preserved as complete entities—that helped to perpetuate tradition.

But the coming of modernism has broken the continuum of tradition. When India gained independence in 1947, the great surge of freedom needed to be expressed in forms that were in themselves free and independent. Modernism was to be the great liberator. It appeared to have just the right associations with progress. The application of logic and rationality to architecture were meant to offset the decadent buildings of the Raj, standing signs of the years of servitude. This new vision was largely imported from the west and entirely alien to the subcontinent. But it was acceptable because it identified neither with a place, nor with a people nor indeed with a discernible ideology. The connections and inspirations were purely technological. The outstanding example of this whole scale importation is Chandigarh, the city designed as a state capital by the French master, Le Corbusier.

When the buildings were complete and people moved in, doubts began to appear on the scale and execution of the endeavour. Could one man—however gifted—design a city for 40,000 foreign clients? Yet Corbusier was as archaic in his design as he was progressive in his methods. Concrete in its unplastered state was brutal to the extreme, and the uncompromising boldness of the shapes he made suggested the coming of something new, indeed something entirely un-Indian. While the buildings of government, the Secretariat, the Assembly and the Halls of Justice were in themselves extraordinarily sensitive buildings—graded in materials and light, designed to reflect the climate and the spirit of their function—as a whole, the city was too diffuse in layout, too severe in material.

Modern residence in South India designed by contemporary architect Laurie Baker.

Chandigarh, the great vision of an acclaimed architect appears today a magnificent folly; a memorial as much to India's new architecture, as a signal to its failure. The buildings that followed were done in the disapproving shadow of the great master. The imitations were purely stylistic and set out to break not just with Corbusier but with India as well. They were the symbols of an Independent India, and so choose to remain anonymous, aligning neither with doctrine nor tradition; they were neither particularly romantic nor exceptionally functional; even their economy was suspect.

Their failure, the failure of modern architecture, was the failure of its buildings to change through the course of their lifespan, to change with the changing circumstances of its inhabitants. The modern Indian architect could not reconcile to change; he did not have the resilience of his ancestors. His building was designed as a final product, an uncompromising blueprint. Improvisation had always been a necessary part of Indian life. Indians have pushed, created, relocated and adjusted with remarkable ease. Such transitions needed acknowledgement in architec-

Above and right : Fatehpur Sikri. Private halls and public pavilions created alternatively intimate spaces and monumentality. The Diwan-e-Khas, above, is in visual contrast to Akbar's pavilion and Anup Talao, right.

ture. The great complexities of traditional building—the streetscapes of Benares, Jaisalmer and Ahmedabad—were based on the principle of growth and accommodation through coaxing and adjustment. In an architecture of cooperation, even encroachment was viewed as positive.

Indian culture was too complex, its demands perpetually changing, too distressingly diverse and pluralistic for an architecture that relied solely on a technological solution. Traditional building, on the other hand produced a setting that allowed for a remarkable assimilation of spatial complexities, idiosyncracies and life patterns. It is this idea which appeals to today's architect. And in some of the projects of the last ten years there seems to be a deliberate shift away from self conscious modernism, to an architecture that synthesizes the old and the new, and scales itself to human values.

Concern for the right kind of image has promoted many Indian architects to seek a valid prototype from history for their new projects. Yet there is always the danger of making too literal a reference to history. It is difficult to distil from the buildings of the past, a column or a bracket that does not become a cartoon of the era. The *chattri,* for instance, in its most fundamental state was an umbrella. The Mughals turned this simple idea into isolated stone pavilions; Rajput architecture moved it to the roof of their buildings, creating on its surface a place of shade. Unintelligent buildings of modern India removed it altogether, or in a fit of selfconsciousness replicated it in a miniature version on their air-conditioned houses, thereby relieving the original idea of any usefulness. The embellishment of urban houses with such historical trivia gives a false, if easy, access to tradition.

Amongst practising professionals at least the realization seems to be dawning: modern architecture in India must change to fulfil the demands of contemporary society.

In many of the older cities where the monotony of the modern has overwhelmed and, at times, obliterated the traditional, there is a growing consciousness of lost values and serious consideration as to how best to adapt them to new building. The associations they make with the past are no longer literal or picturesque, but stem from a distillation of space, of structure. A regionally conscious architecture need not rely on personal whims and obsessions, rather it takes its cues from localized patterns of climate and lifestyles.

Each region has developed its own methods of coping with the peculiar climatic and cultural conditions, and architects throughout India are seeking their inspirations through a regional vocabulary of building. For the examples are still there, speaking a language that has been practised in India for generations. And they speak it still, with a gentleness, a refinement that has been tempered by centuries old tradition and a relentless climate.

Ritual and transformation: the masked dance in India

KAPILA VATSYAYAN

Children throughout the world love wearing masks. The excitement and the stimulation of becoming animal, bird, giant, monster, princess, prince, deity or god, devil or angel, is universal. The paper masks made or bought by children are symbolic of man's universal urge to be able to transform himself. Ancient civilizations at a pre-cerebral or intellection stage have used the mask. They are found in the paleolithic caves of Europe, Africa and India. There is evidence in pre-historic rock cave paintings in India, especially those of Bhimbetka and Mirzapur, of hunters wearing masks. They are close parallels of masks of Africa which can be traced back to pre-historic times, from the caves of Tassili in Hoggar of the Sahara desert as also those of the Bushman rock paintings of South Africa showing hunters with bird masks and animal skins. Similar masks of great antiquity are known to Central Africa, particularly the Cameroons.

Besides there are the undatable Australian masks. Egypt perhaps was the first of the civilizations to recognise the mask in formal ritual. We are told that during Egyptian feasts, masks were used to represent gods and masks were of course placed upon the face of the mummies. Recent exhibitions of Tutenkhamen Relics have displayed spectacular masks made of gold. South America has a rich history of masks from the ancient to the medieval times. Mexico has a vast range of masks representing different deities. Evidence of early stone sculpture from the Maya, Olmec and Aztec civilizations provide considerable evidence of masks of many kinds. In north America masks were the most precious aspects of cultures known to the native American Indians, especially the Hopi, the Pueblo and the Zuni who used them for ritual performances. The Eskimos in Alaska were the creators of highly complex designs and multi-coloured patterns for their face masks.

Asia shares this tradition with the peoples of other continents. In Asia masks have appeared early in each of the cultural areas, Chinese, Indian, Japanese or Indonesian. Bronze masks were used by the Chinese as early as Chau dynasty. In Japan, masks continue to be used in innumerable forms, the most sophisticated of these being the masks of the No Theatre. In India, Sri Lanka, Java, Bali and Nepal, masks have been used as part of ritual and theatre. However, unlike north America and western Europe, in Asia masks are not restricted to those groups

The mask used in ritual performance : a dramatic moment from the dance drama Mudiyettu.

The mask as an archetypal image is seen above in Purulia Chhau. Opposite page : stages in the Kathakali make-up. An example of the full make-up and headdress is seen in the picture, bottom right.

of society commonly called Aboriginal or Tribal. As in Africa, the mask and the act of masking your face is a most important moment of transmutation and transformation. For a child the joy of becoming animal, bird and god is momentary. For an adult the ritual act of wearing the mask to become another (animal, bird or spirit) is a moment of the greatest significance. The actor invokes and collects energies of the primeval forces of nature to contain superhuman power. He is transformed through the mask to become larger than himself. Asian cultures and civilizations have recognised this urge and given it a social status. A theory of aesthetics validates this urge, thus enabling the performer to use the mask with a very high degree of refinement and stylization.

Why and how did this happen? How was it possible for the peoples of Asia to hold a world view over a long period of history which made the wearing of masks central to their culture?

Perhaps one deduction is obvious. Mask and mask like make-up of the face could develop, mature and survive in cultures which, with purpose, subordinated subjective individual emotion. These cultures looked at all like phenomena through archetypal images of the good and the beautiful, the evil and the grotesque, gods and demons, youth and old age, bird and animal, but not with specific particularity of character. Also the mask and mask like facial make-up could be perfected and refined only in cultures which believed in the principle and process of mutation in nature, where one form of organic life could become another, man could be god, and so on. Closely related to the above two concepts, that is, the demand for impersonality and the belief in transmutation and transformation, was another fundamental approach, which relates to the notion of time. Mythical time could become historical actual time, and through ritual performance and spectacle, actual time could become mythical time. This logically led to the creation of great ritual events of specific durations in enclosed spaces, where for that time and duration actual space was transformed into another order of consecrated space.

A recognition of these fundamentals is crucial for understanding and appreciating Asian, and particularly Indian, masks and mask like facial make-up in dance and dance drama.

The entire spectrum of the use of masks and ritual in dance, drama and in great spectacles of the performance of the epics, the *Ramayana* and the *Mahabharata*, is the direct result of this world view and these concepts. Each form has therefore to be understood against the background of the fundamental concepts and within the social context, for outside this context they are just pieces of great decorative skill.

Masked dances are pervasive throughout the Indian subcontinent. They can be seen at the level of tribal society. They are popular in agricultural communities. They are used in the presentation of dance and drama revolving round the themes of the epics, the *Ramayana* and the *Mahabharata*. They are an essential part of the dramatic ritual of the Buddhist monasteries of the upper Himalayas, and they are used in lyrical dances in eastern India.

Behind this vast spectrum of masks and mask like facial make-up, can one discern a pattern or classify them in categories? For facility of description, perhaps we can consider four broad categories.

At the primeval level, the mask is used in a community for religo-magical performances. The dancer or the performer undergoes great austerities, purifies himself,

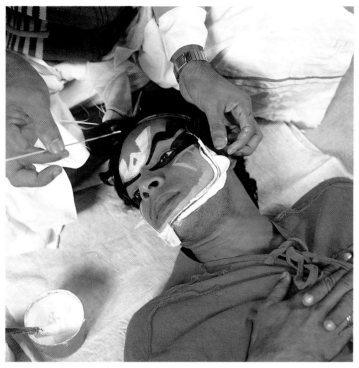
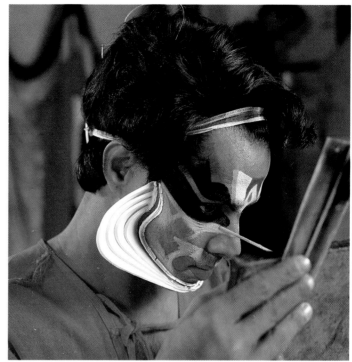
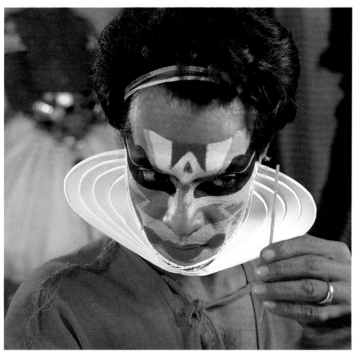

Above and opposite page : masked dances of the Buddhist monastery. The dancers appear as animals, demons or gods to act out a cosmic drama.

undertakes fasts and then adorns a mask symbolizing the abstract forces of nature. Often the spirit of the dead is invoked, at other times the spirit of the tree is invoked and yet other times the spirit of the tutelary deity is invoked. The dancer is a special person: the mask is a sacred object. The moment the individual wears this mask, he is no longer human. He is transformed to superhuman status: he is now prophet, doctor, preceptor combined. For the duration of the ritual, he is empowered by the community to be leader and teacher. He has the fullest immunity to invoke the forces of nature, to offer advice, or punish members of the community. The mask is used as a tool for providing power and authority, and for creating a sense of the supernatural on earth. To this category belong innumerable masks from all parts of India, especially the masks of the Santhals. Communities in southern India, especially Kerala, use facial make-up to achieve the same ends. The most spectacular amongst these are some forms of Kerala known by the generic term Teyyam.

The second category is of masks and mask like facial make-up used in agricultural societies for fertility rituals connected with sowing, harvesting and transplanting of paddy. Agricultural societies in many parts of India perform ritual dances with masks largely for fertility, or to invoke the gods of rain. Here, masks represent all aspects of nature and the performance comprises people wearing masks of trees, birds, animals, showing nature in all its abundance.

The third category are the masks and facial make-up used in ritual performances connected with shrines, temples or monasteries. At this level, the masks begin to represent the malevolent and the benevolent forces of nature, good or evil, beautiful or ugly, dynamic or godly. Such performances can be seen throughout India. The universal principle which provides a thread of unity through all these diverse forms, whether drawn from the Buddhist myths or Indian epics, is the juxtaposition of the good and the evil, the combat between them, and the ultimate victory of the good.

The fourth category is of masks worn on the face as an absolute artistic stylization. At this level, abstraction of emotion is characteristic. The Seraikala Chhau is the outstanding example.

Amongst the innumerable forms of the third category are the masked dances of the Buddhist monasteries of Hemis and Thiksey in Ladakh, performed against the backdrop of snow clad mountains. The courtyard of the monasteries serves as the stage. The two groups of Lamas appear and take their positions. There is the sound of trumpets, music, and the rhythm of the large metal cymbals. Then the masked dancers appear, representing animals, deities and divine beings. After a slow beginning, the whole arena is changed into a mighty battle between the forces of good and evil where the dancers whirl and leap with great dexterity. The arena is transformed into another world. The mask is worn by the Lama as a ritual act, where for that time and duration he loses his identity and becomes animal, demon or god. The silence and the solitude of the monasteries is broken by the sounds of trumpets and gongs, pipes and flutes and the enactment of this cosmic drama by the spectacular masked dancers of the Lamas.

In contrast is the dance drama form called Mudiyettu from Kerala in the south. This is not a Buddhist theme, but taken from one of the Hindu myths where the goddess Kali vanquishes the demon Darika.

Tall trees, dark green shadows, the sunlight playing on fresh paddy fields, the meandering back-waters of Kerala,

are the landscape. Coconut and arecanut palms rise high above, connecting heaven and earth, standing as a symbol of the centre of the earth, the *axis mundi* and the *stambha*, or pillar, of mythologies of all ancient civilizations. An enclosure is temporarily set up, a centre is established, a line is drawn. The Kurup master, through this one line and the centre, creates a figure of goddess Bhadrakali with amazing swiftness and a deftness of touch. Quick strokes outline the head, the torso, the arms and the legs. The outlines are first filled in with primary colours. Other colours are piled upon specific parts to provide volume to the figure, turmeric, burnt coconut leaves for green, the darker hues for black and *kumkum* for red. Before your eyes rises the mighty figure of Bhadrakali come to life through all these colours and cereals. The icon on the ground is not uni-dimensional since the colours are piled one upon the other to define the ornaments and the contours of the huge image of Bhadrakali. The skirt, made of *kumkum* and lime, appears as a rich textured piece of tapestry. The anklets and the ornaments of silver or gold are perfect in design. In her eight arms, the deity holds the diverse weapons of her power. In one of these is the severed head of that demon of demons, Darika. The ritual of drawing the figure on the ground is conducted to the accompaniment of drumming and singing and is com-

pleted to synchronise with the rising crescendo of the drums. Once the image is completed, the *Tantri*, or priest, sits to worship this goddess who is his creation. The idea, given 'form', is brought to life through the recitations of the *Tantri*. The lamp, which is lit in the beginning, is kept aflame by being continually filled with oil. It is the symbol of the beginning and of the consecrated circle reconstructing mythical time. The *Tantri* continues his recitation, the drumming becomes louder and gradually a dance begins, not around the figure but over it. In a wild frenzy, almost as if possessed by the spirit of the goddess, the *Tantri* moves, first carefully, and then madly over the entire figure. In a trance the figure is desecrated. There is no painting left, no image, only the idea and the light of the lamp.

The idea comes to life through being given a concrete form, and the form returns to the formless in the first phase. But the 'energy' released is symbolized by the lighted lamp, which is carried to the second arena of the actual performance. Now it is another group, the Marars, who perform the drama. The singing, the recitation, the performance is the ritual enactment of the myth of the killing of the demon Darika by Kali. As is common in most myths in India relating to power, its limitations and its destructiveness, here too, the story revolves around

Above and opposite page right : the facial make-up of the dance form Yakshagana from Karnataka is determined by character type. Yakshagana uses many categories of make-up. Above right : the mask as the supernatural : the spectacular Teyyam from Kerala.

the demon who sought boons from god Shiva. The demon's austerities and meditation had made him the recipient of these boons. The boon that Darika most wanted was that of immortality. Shiva laughed. "No man should be able to kill me," demanded Darika, "but of woman I am not afraid; it would be demeaning to ask the Lord for a boon to be saved from a woman." So the demon went on to amass power, challenging his enemies in all the directions of the world.

Cosmic balance is now disturbed. The gods plead for help from Shiva. The head of Nandi, Shiva's divine vehicle, emerges from the top of a half-curtain to reassure them. Thereafter the entry of Darika, with torches (*mashals*) lighting up his demon face, painted with the same texture and colours as that of the image, is spectacular and dramatic. He emerges as if from the primeval forces of the environment, the lush trees, the tall forests, the shadows of the coconuts and now, instead of the sun, the moon shimmers through the leaves. Darika runs in

different quarters, eager to hear the cries of enemies whom he will vanquish but he can hear no shouts, except the echoes of his own voice. Then comes a voice from the mountains and the forests, a voice he does not recognise, a voice feeble and feminine, distant but sharp. This is the voice of the goddess Kali, who·challenges the demon. Darika, though not afraid of women, now remembers that Shiva's boon will save him from male but not female foes. He is afraid. Even so, confident of his power, he appears to do battle. Then Kali begins the dance of the powerful energy who crushes the desire for power. As theatrical spectacle, the performance is lightly structured with exits, entries, diagonals, crossings, use of spatial areas, freezing, pauses and blockings. At the level of myth it underpins the eternal theme of power and its limitations.

Darika is vanquished by Kali after a heroic battle, which represents the confrontation of not only good and evil but also that of the desire for power and its limitations. Diverse theatrical expressions are used, ranging from the recited word to the sung word, from a system of questions and answers to singing and drumming. This is supported by large leaps on the ground and in the air, dramatic exits and entries and a fairly developed vocabulary of movement. Fundamental to the performance is the transformation of the face through the mask like make-up. The headgears, of bamboo and coconut, lend an aura of mystery. It is as if the coconut comes to life through these mythical figures. Mudiyettu culminates in a moment of trance, when the actor who plays the role of Kali is possessed with this divine power of the goddess.

The two great epics, the *Ramayana* and the *Mahabharata*, are sources for dance and dance dramas which use masks to portray archetypal characters. The epics have inspired a tradition of masks and mask like facial make-up, a tradition common to India, Thailand, Indonesia and Burma. Again the variety and diversity is bewildering. In the *Ramayana* of Orissa known as the Sahi Jatra, over-size masks are used to present the characters of the epics. Mask like make-up is used in the sophisticated form of Kathakali from Kerala, which compares favourably in its stylization and refinement with Kabuki of Japan. From amongst this vast array we may mention the very special masks used by the Purulia Chhau of eastern India. The Purulia Chhau is an open area performance against lush green background. After an initial ritual lasting six to seven days, the performance begins at night with an invocation to the elephant god Ganesha. The actor who plays this part not only wears a mask but also has an extra pair of artificial arms tied to his back, and thus represents Ganesha as a four-armed deity. The entry of Ganesha is the beginning of the episode. The story then unfolds swiftly with quick entries and exits of other characters, each wearing a mask, to the thunderous playing of the large drums called *dhumsa*. Dancers with masks and headgears appear whirling, swinging, leaping, falling, crawling, running, to create an other-worldly illusion of the combat between good and evil.

In Purulia Chhau, characters from the epics emerge before the spectator in a form of raw masculinity with no lyricism or seeming refinement. The masks are worn close to the face and are strangely realistic in their fierceness, complete with moustaches, teeth, hair lines on the chin and forehead and so on. The mask of the demon Ravana is composed of ten heads arranged horizontally. It calls for great strength and balance for a dancer to go through the leaps and jumps with a mask of this kind balanced on the head. Similarly, Kumbhakarna's mask is truly demonic, profane, wild with hair, snarling mouth, beard, and so on. There is something almost primeval about the masks of Purulia especially when compared to the make-up techniques of the south Indian dance forms. The masks of Rama, Arjuna and Krishna are relatively placid, though here also there is no use of light, soothing pastel shades. They are all seen in royal blue: here is a marked difference between the colour symbolism used in south India and east India, particularly in Purulia Chau. In practically all kinds of the southern dance forms, green or *paccai* is associated with noble men or heroes. In Purulia Chhau, blue becomes the basic colour, possibly because blue was the colour associated with god Vishnu. Shiva wears a white mask. He has a realistic coil of hair, a more realistic coil of snake and the only apparel worn is the deer skin. It is interesting to note that although the gods and goddesses, demons and deities, noble heroes and warriors are the same in different parts in India, their varied representation in each of the regions speaks of a distinctive regional interpretation. The women characters, as in all other

Dancers of Purulia Chhau, wearing the very special masks of this form, leap and whirl in a series of dramatic movements.

dance dramas, are presented naturally and sometimes they have only make-up and do not wear masks, following the same conventions as in Kathakali.

Almost unique to Purulia Chhau is another group of masks; these are the masks of the birds and the animals. In most other dance drama forms of India, masks of animals and birds or anthropomorphic deities are restricted to the face or the head. In Purulia Chhau animals and birds are shown through a complete masking of the body. Thus for example, there is the Varaha or the boar *avatara*. He enters not only with the facial mask of a boar, but also as a dancer on all fours and with a boarskin on his back. Other mythical animals, especially the snake and the tortoise, are represented by characters who crawl on the ground, on their abdomens if necessary. Birds are also

shown with a pair of wings, a head and face mask and a costume which represents the body of the bird. In this respect Purulia Chhau continues a tradition which seems to have died down in other parts of India.

An example of the mask like facial make-up used to portray an archetype is of course the well known form Kathakali. In Kathakali, as also in a connected form, Yakshagana, the principle is to transform the human face deliberately in such a manner as to have no connection with reality. In both Kathakali and Yakshagana, the theme is largely of the *Ramayana* and the *Mahabharata*, but in each the facial make-up is determined by the character type, such as good characters, good characters in anger, evil characters and the real demon characters. Besides these principal types, there is a group of charac-

Above : another dramatic moment from Purulia Chhau, showing the inherent vigour and dynamism of the form. In contrast is Seraikella Chhau (opposite page) whose masks and movements show delicate emotion and lyrical charm.

enclosing line of red. The forehead has a large *tilaka* of red, white and black: the design of the *tilaka* varies from character to character and many a time it is this which helps the audience to identify a particular character. The eyes and eyebrows are enlarged with *kappu* (collyrium). For heroic characters like Arjuna, Yudhisthira, et cetera, black moustaches are painted along with a white or black paint on the chin to suggest a beard. Many variations are possible within this basic design.

The colour of the basic make-up changes in the case of *Raksasas* or demons: now it is red and green. Kathakali also follows the symbolism of red denoting evil and heroism. In Yakshagana, a combination of red and green or blue represents the demons in their moods of valour and fierceness, and red and black in their moods of fierceness and evil. All this when put together, the red and blue combination, the use of an overlayered red and white with a particular design and the large square moustaches, gives a fearsome impression.

Other characters have make-up which is intricate and effective. Indeed, the Yakshagana uses at least eight to ten categories of make-up, which is much more than that of Kathakali.

The variety of make-up is appropriately supplemented with an equally impressive variety in other aspects, such as headgears, jewellery, costumes and the like. Character types are carefully categorised through the different types of headgears, costumes and jewellery.

The last level is the use of the mask not for archetypal characters or emotions, but more to present a placid mood through the mask without using the muscles of the face to communicate sentiments. The outstanding example of this category of art theatre, which uses the mask like living poetry, is the Chhau dance of Seraikala. The masks of Seraikala Chhau are not archetypal characters of good or evil, nor are they abstractions of major emotions of love, hatred, fierceness, disgust, heroism; instead they are lyrical friezes of delicate emotion. The masks of Seraikala are not those of gods and demons of the mythical world, they are masks of the gentle night and the morning, of the sun and the moon, and of ordinary men and women crossing rivers, fishing and hunting. The theme of these dances relate to the sun god, *ratri* (night), dawn (*usha*), a boatman (*navik*), a *dheebar* (hunter) etcetra. The Seraikala masks remind us of the masks of Sunda in eastern Java or the sophisticated masks of the No plays of Japan. In deep contrast to the larger macro movement of the legs as used in Purulia Chhau, and the intricate micro movement of the face in Kathakali, the emotions and delicate sentiments of the Seraikala dance are portrayed through the movement of the lower legs, the waist, torso and the masks. The wearing of the masks enables the dancer to lose his identity, and the process of impersonalisation is common, but this impersonalisation has a deep lyrical charm and quietness of its own. There is an impressive variety of masks as well as the vocabulary of movement of the lower and the upper limbs. Altogether the performance succeeds in creating a charmed atmosphere of a willing suspension of disbelief, and takes the spectator to another world.

The spectrum from the dancer wearing the mask in tribal societies, where he assumes the spirit of the god and is therefore often in a trance, to the sophisticated fluidity of movement as in Seraikala Chhau, is very wide. It is representative of the co-existence of the plurality of approaches, and of the diversity of expression inherent in the masked dances and mask like facial make-up as seen in the dance drama forms of India.

ters like priests, and women, who do not wear masks. The basic colour of the good character is always green in Kathakali; in Yakshagana it is pink-yellow. In Kathakali the good characters in the mood of anger also wear a red facial make-up, and in Yakshagana anger is symbolized with both red and black. The dynamic characters in Kathakali wear very different designs on their face and also have a pith ball on their nose.

In Kathakali, the basic colour for heroes depicting heroism, valour and fierceness is green (*pacca*) while in Yakshagana it is a pink-yellow. The cheek-bones, cheeks and chin are first covered with a basic layer of pink made up by mixing coconut oil, water, rice paste and lime. On this, different designs are drawn to represent different characteristics or moods of the character. For young princes like Nakula or Sahadeva, a large white portion is drawn near the eyes with an inner area of white and an

Indo-Islamic calligraphy: geometry of the soul

AMEENA AHMAD AHUJA

"God has inscribed beauty upon all things"
A sacred Islamic precept.

Indo-Islamic calligraphy acquired a distinct and individual identity as it developed and flourished over the centuries. Though essentially Arabic in origin, calligraphy in its Indian setting became an integral part of the composite tapestry that Indian art values have always represented. It came to play a vital role within the framework of Indian aesthetics. There was a constant interaction between calligraphers and artists, architects and stone carvers, which inspired works of dazzling richness and beauty.

The dictionary defines calligraphy as the art of beautiful writing. It derives from the Greek words, *Kallo's*, or beauty, and *grapho*, to write, that is, the skill imparted to penmanship to raise it to an artistic level. The Arabic word for calligraphy is *Khattati*, derived from Ilm-ul-Khatt—knowledge of script; hence the appendage Khatt before each distinctive style of writing, the Khatt-e-Kufic, the Khatt-e-Sulus and so on. Calligraphy in the Indian language Urdu is *khus-naveesi* or beautiful writing. This is exactly what *Shuji* and *Shodo* convey in Japanese, implying penmanship perfected through Kanji, inspired with the highest discipline in artistic expression, and suffused with content and meaning. This fundamental connection and interdependence between sound and its inherent need to manifest itself as a pleasing visual concept is an important consideration in calligraphy generally and in Islamic calligraphy in particular.

Here it should be remembered that Islam discourages the use of icons and representations of figurative images; thus the artistic urge of its followers was expressed through this non-figural visual art that satisfied both religious and aesthetic needs. The letters of the Arabic alphabet with their upright strokes and full curves, had an inherent geometric structure capable of producing decorative and ornamental designs in a pleasing linear rhythm.

As pure art form, the symbols of Arabic calligraphy have given to the artist-calligrapher the main ingredient used in composition, design, perspective, proportion, that is, the perfect line—the Khatt-e-Kamil in Islamic calligraphy. This explains the relationship between the entire Islamic system of pattern-making and the notion of writing.

The perfect line of the calligraphic symbol involves a study of geometric forms of the letter and the use of the rhombic dot. This dot is all-important. It fixes and as-

Centre of rosette (or shamsa) *which bears the names and titles of Emperor Shah Jehan; Mughál, circa 1645; opaque water colour on paper. Now at the Metropolitan Museum of Art, New York. Purchase, Rogers Fund and The Kevorkian Foundation Gift.*

Above : close-up of a calligraphic panel from the Qutab Minar, Delhi. Right : calligraphy on the Alai Darwaza at the Qutab Minar, Delhi.

certains the relative shape and size of each letter. The standard *alif* is the first letter in the alphabet of Arabic, Persian and Urdu. It is also the first letter in the name of God, Allah. Then there is the standard circle, as in the letter *qaf* which is the first letter of the Book of Revelation, the Quran. The Arab artist-calligrapher Ibn Muqla in the 10th century scaled the *alif* to seven rhombic dots and placed them vertex to vertex. The standard circle of *qaf* with its form like the crescent moon was scaled down to two plus five rhombic dots equalling seven in such a way that the circle made up of five dots stops midway leaving space for two invisible dots. This scale is applied to all the letters of Arabic calligraphy. Ibn Muqla further evolved a precise and sophisticated device to mark out the vowels from the consonants. These are the diacritical marks or vocalisations easily identified by their name and appearance. The rhombic dot, the standard *alif* and the standard circle are the three units which account for the discipline and relationship of one letter to another. This produced some of the most cherished and beautiful linear concepts in calligraphy. It led poets and calligraphers to go into ecstasy over the rounded circular movement of certain letters, and the elongated recumbent aspect of others. The elegance and aesthetic appeal of scripts like the Sulus, the Naskhi, the Rehani, the Nastaliq to mention only a few, explains the poet's ecstasy. Some of these scripts were perfected in India; along with the Kufic, this is especially true of the Sulus and the Naskhi.

In a broad sense calligraphy is the ideal tool for recording and communicating ideas and thoughts. As it developed over a period of time, the art of calligraphy incorporated numerous styles of writing and scripts, as numerous as the master calligraphers themselves. It came to represent one of the richest and most sacred traditions of human cultural heritage. It became a primary form, a visual art with all its inherent intrinsic values.

Before the late introduction of Western printing technology, the function of the calligrapher in Islam was the all-important task of dissemination of spiritual and secular knowledge amongst the believers. It is not surprising that exquisitely calligraphed copies of the Quran became prized possessions, to be recited and often committed to memory. Islamic calligraphy and illumination are the Khattat's homage to the Quran, for the sake of which he revised, invented and constantly searched for new styles and techniques and applied them to diverse materials and surfaces, forever testing his skill. Fine quality paper produced in India, parchment, faience, ceramic, marble, sandstone, metal, precious and semi precious stones such as jade, lapis-lazuli and coral, and ivory were all used for Quranic and other sacred and secular inscriptions. The word calligraphed with rhombic dots and distinct diacritical symbols was the source of joy for the Khattat, and for the patron who commissioned Quranic manuscripts or caused the construction of monuments sacred or secular to be adorned with calligraphic designs. The immense possibilities of calligraphic variety far outstripped those of the printing machine. Even the most perfect attempt of a printer could only perpetuate one transient moment out of that infinity of phases of living expression produced by the calligrapher's reed-pen or brush. Both pen and brush were freely used in India. The ink-covered tip of the reed-pen was allowed to create its magic on a chosen surface. By that very act of application that accompanies the birth of all true works of art, the master-calligrapher triumphed over the flux of time. The heritage he created included illuminated copies of the Quran and the design and composition for monu-

Above : song from an illuminated Dakhni manuscript in Nastaliq script, Deccan, circa 1625-35. Jagdish and Kamla Mittal Museum of Indian Art, Hyderabad.

*Top and opposite page : two views of superb monumental
calligraphy at the Qutab Minar, Delhi.
Right : the exquisite calligraphy of Amanat Khan at the Taj
Mahal, Agra.*

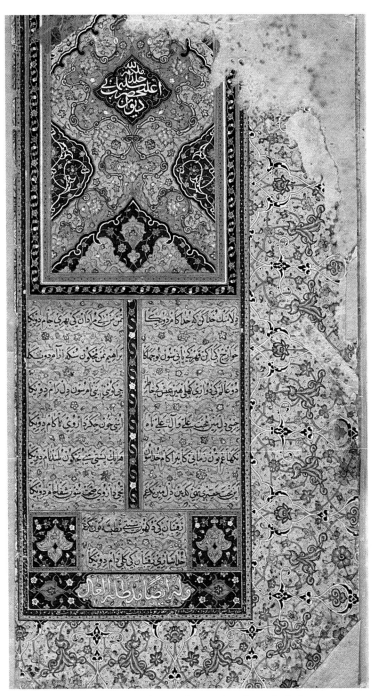

Diwan-e-Sultan Muhammed Quli Qutb Shah manuscript inscribed in excellent Thulth by Maulana Zainuddin Ali Shirazi, Golconda, late 16th century A.D. Courtesy Salar Jung Museum, Hyderabad.
Opposite page : calligraphy as design at the Taj Mahal, Agra.

mental calligraphy. India offers some of the finest specimens in this pursuit. Manuscript and epigraphic calligraphy was produced here by Khattats who amalgamated traditional rules with indigenous concepts.

What guided and motivated the steady progress of calligraphy was evidently the all-consuming love and dedication the artist-Khattat felt for the word of God, embodied in the Quran. Like great art the world over, calligraphy was inspired by, and used in, the service of religion. This was entirely so in the early stages of its formulation and caused its instant acceptance as an art form. The Quran was dictated to scribes by the Prophet as it was being revealed to him. This established calligraphy as a sacred pursuit, a concept supported by texts from the Quran itself. In one *sura* or chapter, God is praised as "He who taught with the reed-pen that which we know not". Another *sura* entitled 'The reed-pen' (Al qalam) gives it the dignity of a sacred tool worthy of being invoked in an oath. This gives to Islamic calligraphy an exalted conceptual status as a art which demands discipline and application. This meant rejection of all that might be haphazard and uncontrolled and that might, therefore, interfere with the purity inherent in the linear aspect of each calligraphic symbol.

The reed-pen, the essential tool for the calligrapher has been poetically referred to as "a cypress in the garden of knowledge." It is eulogised as the miraculous thing, light in weight, heavy in importance. There are numerous chapters in classical oriental literature dealing with the art and skill required in trimming and clipping the desired angle of the tip of the pen. The Khattat himself was respected and honoured as "one who walked across the valley of calligraphy and became famous." In order to successfully cross this valley, however, the Khattat had to undergo long concentrated periods of study with a master, constantly practising, letter by letter. A well known verse says:

"I spent forty years of my life in calligraphy. My hand did not easily grasp the tip of calligraphy's tresses."

If there is humility in those words the following verse expresses pride and satisfaction at a perfect result:

"When your pen draws the perfect letter *dal*,
It surpasses in beauty the tresses and stature of the beloved."

During the years of apprenticeship the pupil-calligrapher learned how to sit properly, squatting or sitting on his heels. He learned to allow the paper to rest on his left hand or on the knee. For larger pieces, however, a low table or desk could be used as if seated at a loom. That is why calligraphy lends itself to comparison with a beautiful tapestry or an embroidered piece.

Perhaps the earliest writing to emerge in Arabic calligraphy was the Khatt-e-Kufic. In its perfect form, Kufic is a precise arrangement of geometric, plaited, knotted, and intertwined lines. And the first Quranic inscriptions were in Kufic as an established liturgical script, therefore, Kufic was to determine the future of Arabic writing and its manifestations in Turkish, Persian and Urdu. As an art form it was known and admired in Europe in the Middle Ages, thus justifying the words that "beautiful penmanship should be a joy to behold even by those who cannot read."

Cursive forms of writing emerged to facilitate legibility as also to satisfy the artistic search for new creative avenues of expression. Some of the earliest Qurans are attributed to the calligrapher Yaqut in India, always handsomely rewarded by one of the Delhi Kings, Mohammed

Above : Wasli by Jawahar Raqam. Courtesy Khuda Baksh Library, Patna.
Opposite page : Khazina - e - Jawahir by the scribe Muhammad Hussain Naqshbandi who transcribed in all major scripts such as Naskh, Kufic, Thulth, Riqa, Nastaliq, Shikasta. Courtesy Salar Jang Museum, Hyderabad.

Tughlaq (13th-14th centuries).

Exquisitely calligraphed and illuminated Qurans from India show how the Indian calligraphers used every opportunity for ornamentation. The headings of *suras* or chapters and the division headings between the Quranic verses were embellished. Ornamentation often spilled across over the margins. In the contours surrounding chapter headings the shapes and forms of the medallions and rosettes employ solar or stellar motifs. Ingeniously conceived, the design of these illuminated islands incorporate the calligraphic contour of a given letter as it merges with the gold, turquoise, indigo or green used as pure colour. Some of the decorative devices are strictly arborescent, in keeping with the divine approval in the Quran for the "perfect tree, firmly rooted, with its branches in heaven." In hands of the Indian calligrapher Ahmed ibn Mohammed this genre is unmistakably indigenous. Apart from using shapes and forms derived from Indian nature, he has employed the Naskhi script. This together with the Nastaliq, the Sulus, and numerous other scripts, was perfected in India. The various decorative forms of writing to emerge from the pens and brushes of Indian calligraphers bear such names as the *Mahi* (fish-like), *Tavous* (peacock-like), *Gulzar* (floral), *Zulf-e-Urus* (bride's lock of hair).

A beautiful specimen of Indian Naskhi appears in the Quran belonging to Tippu Sultan of Mysore. Here the Naskhi script in black ink is arranged on strips of ivory-white with irregular cloud-like edges picked out in old gold. For the *sura* headings and to mark out one verse from another, the Khattat employs the Ruqa script in gold lettering. This arrangement creates perfection of a non-figural visual concept, embodying the Islamic genius for expressing abstract thought in an aesthetic and pleasing manner.

One of the fascinating scripts, distinctly Indian in its development, was the Khatt-e-Shikaste, "the broken script". The Shikaste lines seem to be dispersed over the surface of the page without apparent order. This makes the script look more like a modern graphic than a legible inscription. It can be admired even without being able to decipher it. Some poet calligraphers, Bedil for example, expressed the state of their agitated minds and broken hearts by writing verse in Shikaste without deviating from the calligraphic principles of elegance. Shikaste further intensified the anguish expressed in the verse. The result makes Shikaste look like "the tresses of a bride"–the Khatt-e-Zulf-e-Urus, another favoured script in India used to express lyrical romantic poetry. Yet another script, the Khatt-e-Ghubbar (dust-covered script), could often be used to express sentiments of anger, envy, or pain in a letter to the beloved or the rival in love. Here again the principle of beauty and the guiding rules controlling calligraphy were kept in mind. One exception to this in India was the Bihari script which seemed to ignore the rules and yet produced manuscripts with their own characteristic beauty. Perhaps the skilful use of coloured inks accounted for this.

The inventive pen of the Khattat produced yet another aspect in Indo-Islamic calligraphy, intriguing and fascinating. In the headings of some royal documents in India there was the extraordinary use of Zoomorphic lettering. With humour and ingenuity the long verticals of a letter or the strokes of a diacritical symbol are made to end in a human or animal form, usually outlined in colour. There is another inventive script, the Khatt-e-Nikhian (finger-nail) when the script is engraved with the finger nail on the back side of the paper and subsequently inked.

بسم الله الرحمن الرحيم

اللهم صل على الرسول المقرب

اللهم صل على النجم الثاقب

اللهم صل على صاحب الوسيلة

اللهم صل عليه و على آله و صحبه

و الحمد لله رب العالمين

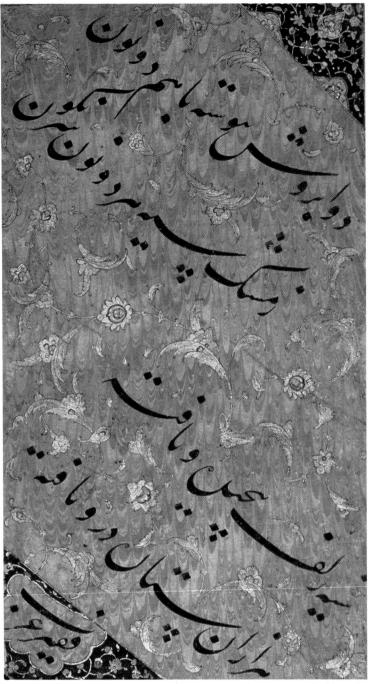

Album page with verses in Nastaliq script inscribed by Fakir Arab, Golconda, circa 1625-35. Courtesy the Jagdish and Kamla Mittal Museum of Indian Art, Hyderabad.

Indo-Islamic calligraphy linked the stylish evolution of indigenous art values with the historical significance of the script and the tools used for writing. These were the reed-pen (*qalam*), the brush, and India ink. The reed-pen and the brush were used in ancient Greece and Rome and also by Oriental people in the Middle Ages. Preference was given to the quill pen in Europe, while countries of the Far East preferred to use the brush. Master calligraphers in India endeavoured not only for fluency in writing, but also endowed the written word with emotional and graphic expression. They brought alive the meaning of the ancient Sanskrit adage "sound must be seen, colour must be heard".

The aesthetic, almost emotional, appeal of calligraphy in the Islamic tradition emanates from the stark, austere and dramatic impact of the immutable sooty blackness of ink on the whiteness of paper or marble. Like the Kanji script of Japan, calligraphy regards black as a colour with diverse and multi-faceted gradations of light and shadow and sees white as an element which enhances these qualities. In the words of Abul Fazl, the historian in Emperor Akbar's court, "the letter of calligraphy is a dark sooty figure to the superficial observer; to the deepsighted, however, a calligraphic letter is a portrait which lays bare the inner soul." This is equally true of *Shodo*.

Calligraphy in manuscripts and on monuments seemed to have been favoured all over India. Monumental calligraphy is seen on mosques, tombs, caravansarais, observatories and so on. These are to be seen in Bhadreshwar and Cambay in Gujarat, in Pandua in Bengal, in Golconda in Andhra Pradesh. The time span ranges from the 12th to the 16th centuries. The calligraphic arabesques are distinguished by intricacy of detail, which enhances the decorative features of all the scripts employed whether Kufic or the cursive scripts. These arabesques, though hewn in stone, reproduce elements from the wooden architecture of the region. In the Deccan the pre-Mughal monuments of Gulbarga, Bidar, Bijapur, Golconda and Hyderabad, have entire facades carved in a technique know as Kashikari where polychrome tiles were used to mark out the calligraphic letter, echoing the surrounding landscape. If in the early stages of its development calligraphy is seen to be stark and austere, in India it progressively became richer in ornamentation. It acquired the quality of musicial notes and seemed to rejoice in the times of splendour and patronage from the rulers of India, the Sultanates, the Mughals, the Rajputs, the Marathas.

A splendid example of Indo-Islamic calligraphy in pre-Mughal India is to be seen on the Qutab Minar (13th century) in Delhi. A tall five-storeyed tapering tower, it is a unique and original architectural example, indigenous in concept using red sand stone, local grey quartoze and white marble. Using the technique of cutting the calligraphic letter in relief directly onto the stone surface, the master calligrapher has inscribed Quranic verses in an impeccable Naskh script. Horizontal carved friezes provide a handsome relief to the plain fluted masonry as they encircle the tower in an upward spiral movement. The tower seems to be adorned with a garland of carved bands exquisitely calligraphed. The fantasy of the arabesques is unique. The tower is an Indian innovation, quite different from the Siah Posh Minar in Afghanistan or the numerous towers in Baghchi Sarai, the capital of the Crimean Tartars.

The enthusiasm for beautiful penmanship made it a more versatile form in Mughal India. The Emperor Babur, himself a poet and a calligrapher, invented the little known Khatt-e-Baburi script and is said to have calligraphed a Quran which he sent as his offering to Mecca. This was in keeping with the standards of education set for noblemen, ministers, theologians, physicians and poets, for whom good penmanship, or at least the knowledge and taste to appreciate it, was desirable together with the art of writing poetry. A story from the Arabian Nights comes to mind in which the king is immensely pleased with the monkey because of his elegant penmanship and his poetic eulogies to the skill of calligraphy.

The Mughal Princess Zebunnisa, herself a poet and a calligrapher, was also a patron of Khattats, poets and scholars. In keeping with Indian custom, calligraphers distinguished by their originality were honoured with high sounding titles, such as "Jawahar Raqam" (Jewel-like letters), "Zarrin Qalam" (Golden Pen) "Ambarin Qalam" (Amber Pen), and so on. It was not a common practice among calligraphers to put their signature on a manuscript or monument bearing their calligraphy. Some names, however, have appeared from time to time, that of Hafiz Nur-ullah and his pupils Sarb Sukh Rai, Nand Ram, Mir Masoum Nami, and Abdul Ghani with his title of Fakhr-e-Bihar (Pride of Bihar).

The pride of all Indian calligraphers and the most celebrated of them all, however, is Abdul Haq Amanat Khan. As the master of calligraphy on monuments, he brought this art to its apex. The finest inscriptions carved out of marble or worked with black inlay on white marble, as in the Taj Mahal, were created by him. Amanat Khan skilfully produces the illusion that all letters are absolutely equal in size, notwithstanding the changing perspective, and the play of light and shadow. If the calligraphic letter is the lamp of wisdom as described by Abul Fazl, then Amanat Khan was truly the master of that lamp.

Unlike other master calligraphers, Amanat Khan has fortunately put his signature on one of the interior walls of the Taj Mahal. His design uses Quranic inscriptions for inspiration and guidance and employs the Sulus, a script which is regular and stately. Its letters are always uniform in thickness of proportion, scaled down to a measure of one-third in the ratio between the straight lines and the curves. Amanat Khan's innovation is his use of overlapping lines of Sulus, where the lines are almost musical in feeling like Bach's use of the contrapuntal technique in his fugues. The overlapping of the calligraphic contours on the facades of the Taj Mahal looks like the juxtaposition of two or more melodies played at the same time, leading to a complete phase. The precise organisation of verticals in rhythmical parallels together with the skilful use of the diacritical signs achieves this. The poetic tribute to a fine piece of calligraphy in earlier centuries was the following:—

As a flower, it would be a rose,
as a metal, pure gold;
as something to taste,
it would be sweet and
as wine it would be pure and old.

This eloquent tribute comes to mind in the presence of the superb calligraphy of the Taj Mahal.

Abul Fazl, the Mughal historian, has defined the written word as far more expressive and elegant than a painted picture. He claims for the calligraphed letter eloquence in its silence, and mobility even though it appears static. While seemingly reclining on a flat surface, it is actually in flight, soaring high. Like earlier calligraphers, he repeats Plato's maxim "Calligraphy is the geometry of the Soul".

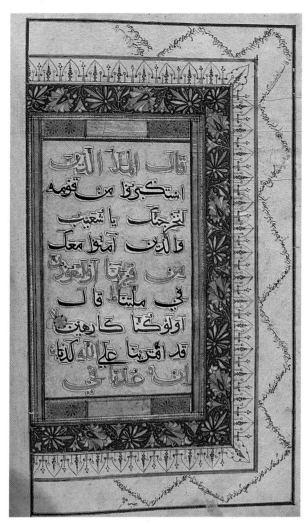

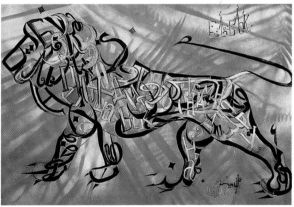

Top : part of the Quran inscribed in excellent Bahar, early 16th century A.D. Courtesy Salar Jung Museum, Hyderabad.
Above : modern calligraphy by the author; "The Optimistic Lion" based on a verse by the Persian poet Hafiz. The calligraphy used is Cyrillic and Arabic.

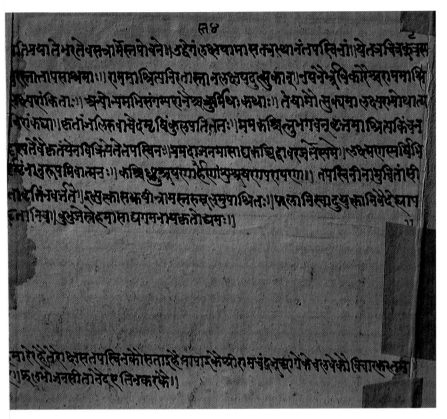

Dharma in the Ramayana and the Mahabharata

P. LAL

The Vedas and the Upanisads, ranging all the way from 5000 B.C. to 1000 B.C., are traditionally considered as "Shruti" or revealed scriptures of Hinduism. This, despite the fact that Song 129 in Mandala X of the Rig–Veda declares:

The Primal Creator, whose eye
controls this world from highest heaven
Whether He made this world, or did not make it,
He surely knows, perhaps he too does not know

In any case, these very ancient texts are songs of wonder and dialogues of idealistic philosophical enquiry; the Vedas are symbolic poetry and the Upanisads are abstract reasoning of a very high order. Hinduism's practical ethics, however, are embodied in the later Kavyas, the two epic narratives, the *Mahabharata* of Vyasa and the *Ramayana* of Valmiki, whose moral message has disseminated over a large part of south-east Asia, particularly Thailand and Indonesia.

The *Ramayana* and the *Mahabharata* are not "dead" epics; they are part of the Indian way of life, having profoundly influenced the way people think and the way they express themselves in song, poetry, drama, and the arts. Valmiki's *Ramayana* is the story of the divine hero, Rama, and his wife Sita, the ideal Indian couple. It tells of their steadfast adherence to dharma, the moral law; of their exile to the forest; of the abduction of Sita by the demon Ravana; and of Rama's pursuit and eventual victory over the demon. It includes miraculous deeds and magical episodes; the hero and heroine overcome trials and tribulations; in the end, truth and goodness prevail.

Vyasa's *Mahabharata* is a rich tapestry of complex and individual characters, who include two groups of cousins who war between themselves. The *Mahabharata* is the story of that war, and the events that led up to it; the epic is a labyrinthine extravaganza of interlocking stories carefully strung into an unmistakable overriding narrative. The heroes and heroines of the epic are subtly, sometimes ambiguously, portrayed, and emerge as characters of great psychological depth and intensity. Within the *Mahabharata* is contained the moral teaching of the Bhagavad Gita, Krishna's message of self-less action to Arjuna, and indeed to the whole world.

The *Ramayana* rouses compassion, the *Mahabharata* an almost cosmic awe. The story of Rama and Sita recommends ideal human love; the story of the Pandavas and Kauravas, the warring factions, is an epic of doom. Valmiki shows the sweet and straight path of dharma, sometimes

Left : Rama and Sita in the forest from a Ramayana manuscript, sub-imperial Mughal School circa 1600 A.D. Courtesy National Museum, New Delhi. Above : reverse of painting.

Dharma in the Ramayana and the Mahabharata

P. LAL

The Vedas and the Upanisads, ranging all the way from 5000 B.C. to 1000 B.C., are traditionally considered as "Shruti" or revealed scriptures of Hinduism. This, despite the fact that Song 129 in Mandala X of the Rig–Veda declares:

The Primal Creator, whose eye
controls this world from highest heaven
Whether He made this world, or did not make it,
He surely knows, perhaps he too does not know

In any case, these very ancient texts are songs of wonder and dialogues of idealistic philosophical enquiry; the Vedas are symbolic poetry and the Upanisads are abstract reasoning of a very high order. Hinduism's practical ethics, however, are embodied in the later Kavyas, the two epic narratives, the *Mahabharata* of Vyasa and the *Ramayana* of Valmiki, whose moral message has disseminated over a large part of south-east Asia, particularly Thailand and Indonesia.

The *Ramayana* and the *Mahabharata* are not "dead" epics; they are part of the Indian way of life, having profoundly influenced the way people think and the way they express themselves in song, poetry, drama, and the arts. Valmiki's *Ramayana* is the story of the divine hero, Rama, and his wife Sita, the ideal Indian couple. It tells of their steadfast adherence to dharma, the moral law; of their exile to the forest; of the abduction of Sita by the demon Ravana; and of Rama's pursuit and eventual victory over the demon. It includes miraculous deeds and magical episodes; the hero and heroine overcome trials and tribulations; in the end, truth and goodness prevail.

Vyasa's *Mahabharata* is a rich tapestry of complex and individual characters, who include two groups of cousins who war between themselves. The *Mahabharata* is the story of that war, and the events that led up to it; the epic is a labyrinthine extravaganza of interlocking stories carefully strung into an unmistakable overriding narrative. The heroes and heroines of the epic are subtly, sometimes ambiguously, portrayed, and emerge as characters of great psychological depth and intensity. Within the *Mahabharata* is contained the moral teaching of the Bhagavad Gita, Krishna's message of self-less action to Arjuna, and indeed to the whole world.

The *Ramayana* rouses compassion, the *Mahabharata* an almost cosmic awe. The story of Rama and Sita recommends ideal human love; the story of the Pandavas and Kauravas, the warring factions, is an epic of doom. Valmiki shows the sweet and straight path of dharma, sometimes

Left : Rama and Sita in the forest from a Ramayana manuscript, sub-imperial Mughal School circa 1600 A.D. Courtesy National Museum, New Delhi. Above : reverse of painting.

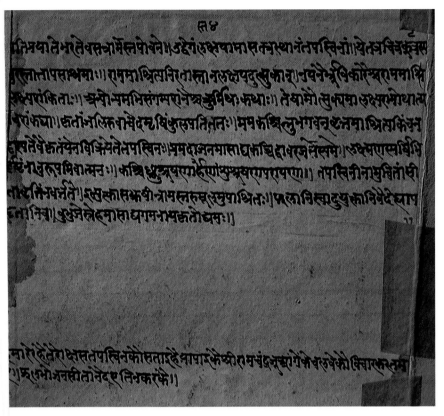

Dharma in the Ramayana and the Mahabharata

P. LAL

The Vedas and the Upanisads, ranging all the way from 5000 B.C. to 1000 B.C., are traditionally considered as "Shruti" or revealed scriptures of Hinduism. This, despite the fact that Song 129 in Mandala X of the Rig–Veda declares:

The Primal Creator, whose eye
controls this world from highest heaven
Whether He made this world, or did not make it,
He surely knows, perhaps he too does not know

In any case, these very ancient texts are songs of wonder and dialogues of idealistic philosophical enquiry; the Vedas are symbolic poetry and the Upanisads are abstract reasoning of a very high order. Hinduism's practical ethics, however, are embodied in the later Kavyas, the two epic narratives, the *Mahabharata* of Vyasa and the *Ramayana* of Valmiki, whose moral message has disseminated over a large part of south-east Asia, particularly Thailand and Indonesia.

The *Ramayana* and the *Mahabharata* are not "dead" epics; they are part of the Indian way of life, having profoundly influenced the way people think and the way they express themselves in song, poetry, drama, and the arts. Valmiki's *Ramayana* is the story of the divine hero, Rama, and his wife Sita, the ideal Indian couple. It tells of their steadfast adherence to dharma, the moral law; of their exile to the forest; of the abduction of Sita by the demon Ravana; and of Rama's pursuit and eventual victory over the demon. It includes miraculous deeds and magical episodes; the hero and heroine overcome trials and tribulations; in the end, truth and goodness prevail.

Vyasa's *Mahabharata* is a rich tapestry of complex and individual characters, who include two groups of cousins who war between themselves. The *Mahabharata* is the story of that war, and the events that led up to it; the epic is a labyrinthine extravaganza of interlocking stories carefully strung into an unmistakable overriding narrative. The heroes and heroines of the epic are subtly, sometimes ambiguously, portrayed, and emerge as characters of great psychological depth and intensity. Within the *Mahabharata* is contained the moral teaching of the Bhagavad Gita, Krishna's message of self-less action to Arjuna, and indeed to the whole world.

The *Ramayana* rouses compassion, the *Mahabharata* an almost cosmic awe. The story of Rama and Sita recommends ideal human love; the story of the Pandavas and Kauravas, the warring factions, is an epic of doom. Valmiki shows the sweet and straight path of dharma, sometimes

Left : Rama and Sita in the forest from a Ramayana manuscript, sub-imperial Mughal School circa 1600 A.D. Courtesy National Museum, New Delhi. Above : reverse of painting.

Winnowing grain in south India.

The greening of India

M. S. SWAMINATHAN

Green plants which harvest sunlight through the process of photosynthesis and produce a wide spectrum of plant products are the primary source of energy in the world. The tropics and subtropics are endowed with considerable "green power" since they are blessed with both abundant sunshine throughout the year and a wide range of climatic and soil conditions which promote considerable genetic diversity in flora and fauna. No wonder then that the tropics and subtropics were the original centres of origin and diversification of most plants of economic value. Agriculture or settled cultivation also began in the developing world. Agriculture in turn made the blossming of culture possible.

Despite all these blessings, India and most developing countries faced serious food problems until recently. This was partly due to the neglect of food crops during the colonial period when there was greater emphasis on crops providing industrial raw material. Soil erosion, non-availability of nutrients, poor irrigation facilities, illiteracy of rural population, unjust agrarian relations, and neglect of rural infrastructure development all retarded agricultural progress. Agriculture was considered in the past to be a profession requiring only brawn and no brain. This is why Mahatma Gandhi said over 50 years ago that Indian agriculture will continue to stagnate as long as the divorce between intellect and labor persists.

Twenty years ago, many leading food experts had expressed the view that India could never become self-reliant in agricultural production. Today, however the country has substantial reserves of food grains. How did this transformation take place?

India became independent in 1947. The memory of the nearly 3 million deaths which occurred during the Bengal Famine of 1943-44 was still fresh in the minds of the public, government officials, and political leaders. As a result, the first Prime Minister of India, Jawaharlal Nehru said in 1948, "Everything else can wait but not agriculture." Such high political priority for agriculture resulted in essential public policy and investment support for food production programmes. A National Extension Service was established as an integral part of the Community Development programme during the period of the First Five Year Plan (1951-56). The aim of the extension service was to help in bridging the gap between potential and actual yields in farmers' fields with the best technology then available.

Progress in achieving self-reliance in food needs was however slow since extension workers did not have much to extend either by way of new knowledge or the inputs neeeded to apply known technology. Compounding the

Modern agricultural inputs such as the use of the harvester (top) and scientific research (above) have increased the Indian farmer's yield. Opposite page : paddy planting in south India.

problem of a growing mismatch between the rates of growth in population and food production, was the incidence of considerable instability in food production from year to year. The fall in production was fairly steep in years affected by widespread drought. Consequently, India had to depend very heavily on imported food grains largely supplied under the PL480 Programme of the USA for balancing its food budget during the sixties. During 1966 and 1967, cereal imports were of the order of 19 million tonnes. The position started gradually changing from the early seventies. By 1972, the Government of India had built up a grain reserve of about 10 million tonnes. Soon, the major challenge became one of enhancing the purchasing power of the rural and urban poor so that the spectacle of large Government grain reserves co-existing with million of undernourished people could be avoided.

I would like to review briefly how the Indian agricultural scenario changed from one of despair in the mid-sixties to one of hope from the mid-seventies onwards.

India's Agricultural Evolution.

During the last part of the 19th century, famines were frequent. The then British Government set up several Famine Commissions which examined the reasons for stagnation and violent undulations in agricultural production. Based on the recommendations of the Bengal Orissa Famine Commission, a Department of Agriculture was set up in the different provinces. In 1928, a comprehensive review of the state of Indian agriculture was made by the Royal Commission on Agriculture. The Royal Commission recommended the establishment of an Indian Council of Agricultural Research (called at that time the Imperial Council) for the purpose of stimulating and supporting research relevant to the improvement of the productivity and stability of production of the major farming systems of India.

During World War II, food scarcity became acute particularly after the occupation of Burma by Japan. Burma was a traditional supplier of rice to India. The Bengal famine was not just the consequence of acute food shortage but the result of the inability of Government to ensure equitable distribution of the available food in an atmosphere of scarcity. The then Government of India launched a "Grow More Food" campaign in 1943, in response to the urgent need for steping up food output.

India is a large country with a wide range of growing conditions. The British economist, Joan Robinson, once wrote that whatever is written about India, if the opposite is written, both may be true depending on the area one has visited. Even today, this statement continues to remain valid since on the one hand, there are States like the Punjab where the average yields of crops compare with the best in the world and on the other, there are areas in the country where productivity as well as methods of production have remained relatively unaltered for centuries. Remedying regional imbalances in agricultural development has hence been accorded importance in the Seventh Plan (1985-90) in development terms.

For the sake of convenience, I would like to recognise three major evolutionary phases. The first phase, extending from 1900 to 1950, was a period of stagnation in our agricultural and rural economy. The average growth rate in agriculture during this period was about 0.3%. Agricultural stagnation meant rural stagnation, and this in turn led to the drain of both brain and resources from the village to the town. The neglect of rural areas was so great that at the time of Independence, most villages did not have even

one source of safe drinking water. Even now there are nearly 200,000 villages which are yet to be provided with potable drinking water. Stagnation also meant that no attempts were made to provide any form of commercial energy in support of agricultural occupations.

Whenever agriculture failed due to unfavourable weather, famine conditions prevailed. This is why considerable thought was given in the pre-independence days to the development of Famine Codes and Scarcity Manuals. Above all, colonial rule tended to freeze social evolution. There was total social failure in the fields of redistribution of agricultural assets like land and livestock and in the prevention of exploitation of primary producers at both the production and post-harvest phases of farm operations.

The second phase of our evolution covering the period 1950 to 1980 was one of growth in the development of the infrastructure necessary for the modernisation of agriculture. The outmoded land tenure system at last received attention, resulting in a gradual elimination of the *Zamindari* and other intermediary tenures. Impressive progress took place during this period in developing powerful instruments for technology development, technology transfer and technology sustenance. The Indian Council of Agricultural Research, the network of Agricultural Universities and several associated institutions in the country provided an effective mechanism for carrying out location-specific research and for developing appropriate technologies to suit different agro-ecological, socio-economic and socio-cultural conditions. Technology transfer mechanisms included the development of extension networks supported by input delivery systems. For sustaining agricultural advance, policy and operational instruments such as the Agricultural Prices Commission and Food Corporation of India were developed.

We can see three distinct trends during the period 1950-80, in terms of programme development. The first major step in promoting accelerated agricultural advance was taken in 1961 when the Intensive Agricultural District Programme (IADP) was initiated. This programme was designed to maximise production in areas endowed with irrigation facilities. Later the introduction of high yielding varieties of seeds was superimposed over the area approach, since the earlier strains did not respond to higher levels of nutrition and irrigation. Through the High Yielding Varieties Programme (HYVP) the missing link in the package programme (IADP), namely genetic strains which can respond well to the rest of the rest of the package, was provided. The area approach was also structured to meet specific ecological conditions like drought-prone, hill and desert areas. The area and crop-centred approaches, however, were found to be inadequate for the purpose of enabling the economically handicapped sections of farmers to take to new technology. It is this lacuna which was attempted to be remedied through the introduction of special programmes for small and marginal farmers, agricultural labour and tribal people. Thus, gradually an individual farmer-cum-specific area model of programme development was born.

Infrastructure development during the period 1950-80 has been particularly impressive in the fields of agricultural research and education, irrigation, fertilizer production and in the storage and distribution of grains. Credit systems for the rural poor were also improved. As a result of the various steps taken during this period, the growth rate in agriculture rose to about 2.8 per cent per annum, thus keeping slightly above the growth rate in population. Also, land use patterns, which were predominantly based on the home needs of the farming family, tended to shift

Scientists and farmers collaborate to improve production. Top : soil sampling in Udaipur. Above : crop research at Hyderabad.

towards market requirements.

The third phase of India's agricultural evolution during this century started with the Sixth Plan in 1980. Besides efforts in sustaining and expanding the production gains already made in crops like wheat and rice under irrigated conditions, the major thrust during the remaining years of this century will be to:

a) Minimise regional imbalances in agricultural growth and make agriculture a powerful instrument of producing more and better quality food, more jobs and more income;

b) Improve the production of pulses, oilseeds and horticultural crops and pay greater attention to post-harvest technology;

c) Accord priority in resource allocation to economically handicapped farmers and landless labour families and to ecologically disadvantaged areas, such as drought-prone and flood-prone areas;

d) Improve the consumption capacity of the rural and urban poor through the generation of greater opportunities for on-farm and off-farm employment; and

e) Design production programmes on considerations of ecological and economic sustainability and for this purpose, strengthen institutions which can promote the harmonious growth of crop husbandry, animal husbandry, fisheries and forestry.

Elements of Agricultural Policy

The major element of the agricultural policy can be described under the following three operational categories:

a) Development of technological packages suited to the diverse agro-ecological and socio-economic conditions of the country.

b) Development of a package of services designed to enable all farmers, irrespective of the size of holding or innate input-mobilizing and risk-taking capacity, to take to new technologies.

c) Public policies to stimulate and sustain production by small farmers on the one hand and to improve consumption by the poor on the other.

Experience shows that only when appropriate packages of technology, services, and government policies are developed in a mutually supportive and reinforcing manner, agricultural expectations become a reality. In fact in India, it has taken a long time to reach a satisfactory state of synthesis of these packages. It is only during the Sixth Five-Year Plan period that we have started observing the full impact of such a symphonic approach to agricultural development.

To summarize, the annual growth rates in agriculture during the three phases I mentioned earlier have been of the following order.

I. 1900-1950 - 0.3 per cent
II. 1950-1980 - 2.8 per cent
III. 1980-1985 - 3.9 per cent

Let me deal with the three major ingredients involved in the evolution of Indian agriculture from a period of stagnation to its present symphonic state.

A. Package of technology

Farming systems and practices have evolved over centuries, and what are usually referred to as traditional systems of farming are the ones which have evolved through observation and experience to suit specific agro-ecological conditions. Such systems of farming are however generally not intended to raise crops or farm animals for the market. When the process of modernization sets in, the principal catalyst is opportunity for remunerative marketing. When food crops are grown for the market, the distinction between them and traditional cash crops vanishes. For example in several parts of India, wheat or rice is the principal cash crop for numerous farming families.

Market-oriented agriculture requires for its success a high degree of efficiency both at the production and post-harvest stages. The goal is to achieve the highest yield possible per units of land, water, time, and labour. This is where improved technologies become essential.

During the first 20 years after India's independence, production advances were achieved largely by increasing the area under cultivation. With growing population pressure, this pathway of increasing production could only lead to a blind alley. Productivity improvement and higher intensity of cropping became necessary to produce the food needed for the growing population.

One of the first tasks therefore became the building up of the scientific infrastructure essential for stimulating and sustaining rapid agricultural advance. Agriculture is by and large a location-specific vocation and therefore a dynamic national research system is a must for sustaining a dynamic production programme.

India is fortunate to have an excellent network of agricultural research institutes and universities. At the national level, the Indian Council of Agricultural Research supports and coordinates scientific research, training, and extension education in crop husbandry, horticulture, animal husbandry, fisheries, and agro-forestry. ICAR is a unique organization since it has concurrent responsibility for both research and education.

Research programmes are carried out in a large number of Central and State research institutes and national bureaus such as the National Bureau of Soil Survey and Land Use Planning, and National Bureau of Plant Genetic Resources. Linking the Agricultural Universities and Central Institutes are the All-India Coordinated Research Projects. These projects bring together scientists working in different institutions and disciplines into a symbiotic partnership. The individual strength of the different research institutes may vary but the collective strengths of All-India Coordinated Research Projects are considerable. Once improved technologies are developed by scientists, verification of the experimental findings in farmers' fields becomes essential before they are recommended for widespread adoption.

ICAR had developed the following methods of demonstrating and verifying new experimental findings in farmers' fields:

a) *"Lab to Land"* programme which aims at extending new experimental findings in the fields of small farmers;

b) *National demonstrations* which are designed to serve as windows into the world of high yield awaiting the farming community; and

c) *Whole-village or watershed operational research projects* which can help to identify the major constraints responsible for the gap between potential and actual farm income.

Since illiteracy is still widespread, ICAR organized all over the country Farm Science Centres (Krishi Vigyan Kendra) for imparting the latest technical skills through "learning by doing."

The personnel policies of a research organization are extremely important to attract and retain dedicated and high quality staff. ICAR introduced in 1974 an Agricultural Research Service (ARS) for the purpose of providing job security and opportunities for promotions even without the occurrence of vacancies. A national Academy of Agricultural Research Management was set up in Hyderabad to provide opportunities for in-service training to the members of the agricultural research service and to promote a scientific culture within the organization.

Agricultural research institutions and universities have identified themselves with the problems of farmers, and farmers often spend many hours visiting the experimental fields and discussing with scientists problems of mutual interest.

Technology development has been based on attention to individual factors of production as well as to farming systems as a whole. In summary, the Indian Council of Agricultural Research has been able to achieve the following:

a) Bring about a close integration of research, training, and extension education;

b) Develop a national grid of cooperative experiments bringing together scientists from different disciplines into working partnership to achieve specific research goals;

c) Bring about close linkages between research and development agencies;

d) Involve farmers as partners in the refinement and testing of technologies; and

e) Introduce personnel policies to promote life-long specialization in remote and often neglected areas.

Let me give two examples of how the research system responded to a specific challenge. After Independence, fertilizer production began within the country with the establishment of fertilizer factories, both in the private and public sectors. Hence, the programme of popularizing fertilizer use in farmers' fields was started using low doses of about 20 kg of nitrogen per hectare in the fifties. Statistical analysis of the data collected from a very large number of trials conducted all over the country showed that there was no economic response even to this low level of nitrogen application. Hence in the early sixties, research on the breeding of varieties which could respond well to water and fertilizer application was started. Thanks to the introduction of semi-dwarf wheat varieties from Mexico through the help of Dr. N.E. Borlaug, suitable strains which could respond well to good soil fertility management were identified within a short period of time. In fact, the semi-dwarf varieties spread from about 4 ha in 1964 to about 4 million ha in 1970. From a peak production of about 12 million tonnes in 1964 before the introduction of high yielding varieties, wheat production in 1986 exceeded 46 million tonnes.

The next example I would like to take is rice. Rice accounts for about 40 per cent of the total food grain production in the country. Its production has increased from 20.6 million tonnes in 1950-51 to 60.10 million tonnes in 1983-84 (data relate to milled rice). During 1985-86, rice production is expected to range from 61.5 to 62.0 million tonnes. Here again, there was stagnation both in production and in yield per hectare until the introduction of genetic strains in the mid-sixties, which had the capacity to respond to good soil fertility and water management. Rice is predominantly a crop of the

Above : fertiliser plant provides a major input for modern agriculture. Opposite page : laboratory research yields valuable data.

southwest monsoon period (i.e., May to October) when problems of pests together with difficulties in water control create difficulties in increasing yield. Fortunately, the All India Coordinated Rice Project of the ICAR, which is a cooperative network of rice research institutions in the country and which works in partnership with the International Rice Research Institute, helped to provide location-specific varieties and technologies for different parts of the country speedily. Non-traditional rice areas like the Punjab and non-traditional rice seasons like the summer season became important in rice production thanks to new technologies. Even in severe drought years, Punjab has maintained high rice yields because of the steps taken by Government to provide adequate energy to pump water from tube wells.

To sustain yields at high and stable levels, we need effective monitoring and early warning systems, particularly with regard to soil, plant and animal health. We are dealing in agriculture with dynamic conditions, and eternal vigilance is the price of a progressive and stable agriculture. To cite an example, in the Punjab, hardly any economic response to phosphorus application was observed in the sixties. In the early seventies, however, phosphorus application became a must to get returns from the applied nitrogen. In a few years, zinc deficiency became widespread. Thus, when farming practices shift from a low to a high productivity level, several new problems relating to plant and soil health confront us from time to time. This is where location-specific research capability becomes vital for sustained progress.

The national goal of agricultural research is the improvement of the productivity, profitability, stability, and sustainability of the major farming systems of a country. Sustainability has to be viewed from the ecological as well as economic angles. We cannot allow depreciation in the basic agricultural assets of land, water, flora, and fauna. While ecological sustainability is basic to the future of agriculture, economic sustainability at a given point of time and place becomes vital for generating the interest of farmers in producing more. An effective national agricultural research system therefore should look at both ends of the spectrum. Improving productivity without detriment to the long term production potential of the soil and economic viability resulting in a satisfactory "take-home income" for the farmers are both essential. This calls for biological and social scientists working together as a team.

B. Package of services

There would be no difference between research of applied value and "ivory tower" research if arrangements were not made for transferring the new technologies to the fields of farmers. In most countries of South and South-east Asia where the average size of a farm holding is usually less than one hectare, the cooperation and assistance of at least a million farming families will be needed to produce an extra million tons of wheat, rice or other cereals. Therefore, no production target can be achieved without first asking the question—"Why should farmers produce more and how will they produce more?"

If this question is asked first, before preparing a development project, we can get our priorities straight. We can then design a system to provide the package of services essential for all farmers to take advantage of new technologies In India, both government and private agencies have been active in providing inputs like seeds, fertilizer, pesticides, and very importantly, credit. Government policies in the development of effective input supply services have evolved over a period of time. Public sector companies like the National Seeds Corporation and credit institutions like the National Bank for Agriculture and Rural Development have become very important instruments enabling small farmers to take to new technologies.

Mass media, particularly radio and the local language newspapers have been extremely important in the dissemination of agricultural information. Television is increasingly becoming a powerful communication tool. Extension services including the Training and Visit (T&V) system of structured knowledge transfer has grown in capacity and effectiveness.

The major goal of the input supply system is to render new technology accessible to *all* farmers. Equality of opportunity in access to appropriate technology should be the foundation of agricultural extension and development planning. Knowledge and skill transfer systems, and the methods of providing the inputs essential for converting knowledge into field accomplishment, must be synchronized in space and time. Also, it is important that the input delivery systems are tailored to suit specific sociocultural conditions.

In recent years, a system of rigorous monitoring of the availability of key inputs in remote areas has been introduced. This system involved getting a checklist of essential activities verified at the village level during a specified fortnight, usually several weeks before the due date of sowing. The organization of an Input Supply Fortnight is a good method of monitoring the input distribution system and identifying weak spots. In other words, such a methodology serves as an early warning system in the area of input availability so that critical bottlenecks can be removed before the onset of the sowing season.

C. Package of Government Policies

Even if good technologies are available and the input supply system is efficient, farmers will not be able to derive benefit from them unless some basic steps are taken by Government. The first area of action is in the realm of land reform. Farmers will have to have a long-term stake in the land for investing in the infrastructure essential for sustained productivity. Security of tenure, land ownership pattern, and the size of the farm holding are all areas which need attention.

In the past, land use decisions were taken by farming families largely based on the home needs of the family and the immediate neighbourhood. With the modernization of agriculture, farmers produce foodgrains and other commodities not only for themselves, but more importantly, for the market. When this transition takes place, opportunities for producer oriented and remunerative marketing become essential for sustaining and stimulating farmers' interest in modern technology.

Input-output pricing policies become crucial. The turning point in Indian agriculture took place in 1964, when the Government of India set up an Agricultural Prices Commission to recommend minimum prices for food grains essential to provide an incentive to the farmers. The Food Corporation of India was also set up to assure the farmers the minimum price announced by the Government. Announcing support price alone will have no meaning unless the Government has the capacity to honour its commitment to the farmers, so that they do not have to sell at prices below the floor price. The Government of India has honoured its commitment to farmers by purchasing all the surplus grain offered to Government agencies by farmers. This is the reason why there are fairly substantial grain reserves now with Government.

I have briefly dealt with some of the major ingredients involved in the greening of India. Essentially the message from the Indian experience is the following:

a) Develop a strong national research capability in agriculture which can help to provide optimum returns from the land, water, livestock, and capital resources available to the country on a sustainable basis;

b) Develop methods of transferring know-how and skills to farmers and provide them with the inputs necessary for converting technological advances into production grains;

c) Introduce agrarian reform, rural development and communication, input-output pricing policies and other programmes which can stimulate and sustain the growth of market-oriented farming;

d) Stimulate consumption by the rural and urban poor by various measures including Food for Work and Employment Guarantee projects; and

e) Consider agriculture not just as a means of producing food for the urban population but also as a powerful instrument of increasing income and employment. Such an approach is essential for generating diversified opportunities for enhancing the purchasing power of the rural population.

The process of the greening of India has just started. The Indian farmers have shown that, whether literate or illiterate, they will adopt new technologies speedily and efficiently provided the technologies are economically viable and socially compatible. The challenges ahead are great. There is need for the ecological rehabilitation of vast areas in the Himalayas. There is need for the scientific upgradation of degraded and wasted lands and waters. Fortunately, the political will and the necessary professional skill are available for sustaining and expanding the greening movement. Green power is the most important asset of rural India. We should intensify and expand our efforts to use this power to convert on a sustainable basis our natural assets into wealth meaningful to our people.

Wildlife in India

M. KRISHNAN

India has been renowned from time immemorial as the storehouse of wildlife, and from remote times its flora has been as highly valued as its teeming fauna. Sages established their hermitages in the forest, far from the fret and bustle of civic life, and Ashoka's edicts (*circa* 300 B.C.) specify the protection of forest trees. This is specially significant considering that it is only quite recently that international wildlife conservation has realised and specified that an integral and basic part of the wildlife of any region is its native, uncultivated flora.

Probably India is the richest in the world in flowering plants. However, no account of its vivid forest flowers and superlative timbers is attempted here, for it cannot avoid botanical jargon and this is a nontechnical survey—a survey only of the faunal part of the country's wildlife.

It is universally recognised that India was the country where wildlife conservation had its origin. It is the land of the Buddha and Mahavira, where the hunting of animals was proscribed by Ashoka's imperial decree. But to know how long and deeply sympathy for wild creatures has imbued life in India, one must turn to the common people. For centuries in south India, water-birds nesting in close company in rustic locations have been zealously protected by the villagers, out of realisation of their singular vulnerability to predation during the three months of their breeding enterprise. There are still many such colonies in the southern countryside, protected solely by the villagers. And in the north, at Bishnoi settlements, crop-raiding animals are not harmed, but vigilantly protected against all hunters.

During the British rāj, shikar or hunting became a popular pastime, when formerly it had been the privilege of a few. Laws were promulgated then to protect some endangered animals, but trapping, netting and snaring by professional pelt and meat hunters went largely unchecked. Many animals were reduced to rarity where they had been common, and one major predator, the Cheetah or Hunting Leopard, became wholly extinct in India. In many princely states wildlife was better conserved in game preserves, where only a few could hunt.

However, it was in the decades immediately following independence and the merger of princely states with federal India that wildlife depletion became a serious threat to the natural integrity of the country. Wood poachers and meat hunters grew increasingly depletive, and the indiscriminate shooting of wild animals gained force. But the main cause of this great decline was the invasion of every kind of wildlife habitat by human occupation and enterprise, by a vastly increased and still growing population, and governmental efforts to provide for this population.

The setting up of the Indian Board for Wildlife in the fifties was the first landmark in governmental cognizance of this great decline. This was a central advisory body,

The superb horns and dark coats of the mature male blackbuck are seen in this picture.

and forests and wildlife were entirely in charge of the governments of the different states of India. The Wildlife (Protection) Act of 1972, and the Forests (Conservation) Act of 1980 were significant steps whereby the Union or Central Government gained concurrent jurisdiction over the country's fauna and wildlife habitats. The inauguration of Project Tiger in 1973 was another major step—this, as well as other success stories in India's wildlife effort, may be dealt with while considering its fauna. Now for a quick, overall look at its bewilderingly rich fauna.

What is distinctive about India's fauna, what sets it apart from other wildlife-rich continents like Africa and South America? Some of its major animals are not found anywhere else in the world. Moreover, two large mammalian families, the cat and deer families, have their largest number of species only in India. Furthermore, many animals of south Asia attain their best development, or largest populations, within India. Lastly, the country's fantastic variations in terrain and climate favour a most exceptional diversity in plant and animal life.

The lesser life, the insects, molluscs, crustaceans, fishes and even amphibians, is so multitudinous and regional that it is left out of this account. Here, only the common wild mammals and some of the vast numbers of birds will be mentioned but even with such omissions the text will have to be tight.

The Hoolock Gibbon of Assam and farther north-east is India's only ape. All its monkeys are either macaques (stocky, with well developed muzzles and cheek-pouches, and omnivorous) or langurs (reachy in build, flat-faced and with no cheek-pouches, arboreal and vegetarian). The Stumptailed, Pigtailed and Assamese macaques belong to the far north-east. Only two macaques have a wide distribution in India, the Rhesus in the north and the Bonnet Monkey south of the river Godavari. The rhesus, olive-grey, short-tailed, pink-faced and with the fur of its lower back characteristically rufous, is the familiar monkey of pilgrim centres and markets in the north. The bonnet monkey replaces it in the south, also grey and pink-faced but with a long tail and more arboreal: the hair on its crown is arranged in a radiating pattern—hence its name.

The last and most notable Indian macaque is the Lion-tailed Monkey of the Western Ghats sholas (close-grown belts of lofty trees peculiar to the southern part of the Western Ghats). It is a glossy black and not liontailed, but certainly has a mane like a lion—a great grey mane sur-

Opposite page : the bulk and power of the great Indian rhinoceros is seen in this picture. Above : a tigress and her cubs relax in water. Left : a herd of swamp deer move in the jungle.

Above : the Indian elephant, majestic and awesome.
Opposite page : a Himalayan black bear peeling off the bark of a tree.

rounds its black face. It is the most arboreal and most predatory of the macaques, feeding on leaves, buds, and fruits and also hunting insects, reptiles and even small mammals actively. Because it was unprotected in its remote sholas it was much poached, and later human invasion of its limited habitats further depleted it. Now it is probably the most endangered purely Indian mammal—the liontail, as also the bonnet monkey, are found *only* in south India.

The beautiful Golden Langur and the Capped Langur are restricted to parts of Assam in the north-east and near around. The black-faced, grey-coated Common Langur is the only monkey found all over India, in some 15 regional races—it is also found outside the country. The black Nilgiri Langur is the only member of its tribe that is exclusively Indian: like the liontailed macaque, it is also restricted to the southern reaches of the Western Ghats, and was also much depleted by being hunted. But its numbers are now reviving with better protection and the expansion of its territory by its taking to the more open forests around the sholas.

Although the Cheetah became extinct within the country, India is still the richest in its large and lesser cats. The Asiatic Lion, the Indian Tiger, the Leopard, the Snow Leopard in Kashmir and the Clouded Leopard in the sub-Himalayan north-east are its great cats. The lesser cats include the powerful Fishing Cat, the Golden Cat of the north-east and the Caracal of the north-west (all three sizeable), the Jungle Cat and the beautiful Leopard Cat all over, the Desert Cat in the arid north-west, the rare Marbled Cat of Assam and the Rustyspotted Cat of south India.

The Asiatic Lion differs in some particulars from the African, and is the lion of the Bible and Persian lyrics: it was distributed widely over west Asia and north India formerly. It perished everywhere else but was saved in the Gir forest of Gujarat by dedicated conservation. Today Gir is the only place on earth where the Asiatic lion is still to be found, a notable feat of conservation begun in the days of the princes and still sustained.

The Tiger, in several regional races, has a wide range over Asia, but it is India that has always been celebrated for this most magnificent great cat, and where it has its main population. It is there all over the country, but with ubiquitous hunting over centuries and, more recently, human invasion of its habitats, even here it became gravely endangered. Realising that the conservation of a particular animal was best done by trusting nature to maintain its balance in an adequately large tract and protecting the entire tract, Project Tiger was inaugurated in 1973 with the setting up of 9 Tiger Reserves in very different parts of India. The project succeeded so well not only in reviving the tiger but also the entire flora and fauna of each reserve that it has now been extended to 15 Tiger Reserves. From Ashoka's days the lion had been the imperial emblem and later the emblem of independent India, but the tiger has now taken its place as the National Animal.

White tigers are not true, pink-eyed albinos but are albinotic, with ice-blue eyes. Though formerly shot in a few places, it was only in Rewa in Madhya Pradesh that it was successfully bred in captivity, and all white tigers in zoos today are from this Rewa stock.

The Panther or Leopard (both names denote the same animal) has a wide range over Asia and Africa, and is the most varied of the great cats. In India, and elsewhere in south-east Asia, a melanistic variety, the black leopard, also occurs in dark forests, but is uncommon. Though less than half the size and weight of the tiger or lion, the

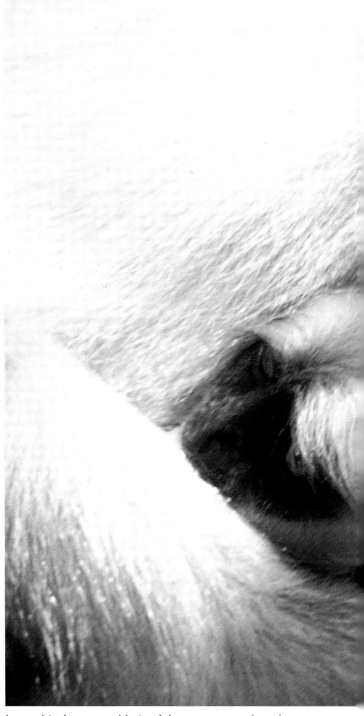

Above : an Indian bear. Above right : the beautiful golden langur of north east India.

leopard is the most athletic of the great cats and can leap and climb as the others cannot—which is why it is never displayed in a zoo in a moated, open-air enclosure as tigers and lions are.

Quite a few kinds of civets and mongooses inhabit the scrub jungles and forests. The Stripenecked Mongoose of the southern hill forests and Sri Lanka is the largest of Asiatic mongooses. The Ratel or Honey Badger, and the Striped Hyena, are two of the few animals that India shares with Africa.

The Jackal, plentiful till recently and now uncommon, the vanishing plains Wolf, races of the European red fox in sub-Himalayan tracts and the dinky little Indian Fox (peculiarly Indian), and the chestnut-coated Dhole (the so-called Wild Dog) are the members of the dog family. The pack-hunting dhole is the main predator after the three great cats.

The Brown Bear in the higher elevations and the

Himalayan Black Bear in the foothills of the mountain range are the Indian races of these widely distributed bears. But *the* bear of the country is the Sloth Bear, once common all over but now rare, a great character of the rocky hill forests that is exclusively Indian.

The rodents and their kin are the most numerous and widely-spread of all mammals, and India has its fair share of them—field mice and rats, Himalayan marmots, big hares of three races, the prickly Indian porcupine, and squirrels. The diurnal Giant Squirrel of the tree forests is one of the largest of all squirrels and the handsomest: the nocturnal Large Brown Flying Squirrel is a trifle larger, and there are lesser flying squirrels. The commonest wild beast of the country is the pretty little Striped Palm Squirrel that haunts human settlements everywhere.

The Asiatic Elephant (which belongs to a different genus altogether from the African) is found in neighbouring countries as well, but India is, and has always been, its

stronghold. Ganesha, the all-important Hindu god, whose blessings are traditionally invoked on all important occasions, is the only elephantine divinity in the pantheon of any religion. From remote times the capturing of wild elephants and their training to serve men in war and peace, for work and pageantry, has been in use in India. Elephants are the largest land animals and highly gregarious: they range far in their feeding and need extensive stretches of unbroken forests. The cutting up of the hill forests by human enterprise has handicapped them severely, but in some southern preserves the great beasts may still be seen in a wholly natural setting.

The saving of the Great Indian Rhinoceros is a saga of dedicated effort. Because of superstitious belief in the magical properties of their horn and flesh, rhinos everywhere are relentlessly poached, and at one time the Indian rhinoceros was reduced to about 20 animals. Today there are over a thousand, mainly in Assam with a

Top : a panther relaxes on a tree. Above : the gaur, one of the world's largest wild oxen. Right above : an example of Indian avifauna. Right below : lion cub in the Gir forest. Far right: the slender loris is found only in the Western Ghats of India.

few in West Bengal.

India has both the largest wild bovines in the world. The Wild Buffalo (dominantly Indian, though it has gone from here to other countries) is a huge, aggressive animal: once it was common in many riverine grasslands but is now confined mainly to Assam. The Gaur, tallest and handsomest of all wild oxen, is also found in other south Asian countries, but has its main population and widest distribution in India, and attains its most magnificent size in the Western Ghats.

Many wild sheep, goats and goat-antelopes belong to the Himalayan ranges within and outside India, but the Nilgiri Tahr is a wild goat peculiar to the craggy hilltops of south India.

Africa is the land of the antelopes, with almost 80 different species. India has only four, but all are remarkable. The Chinkara is a variety of the Persian gazelle, and favours dry, ravine-cut forests. The Blackbuck, which roamed the plains in vast herds, has been sadly depleted by hunting and is now uncommon. The black-and-white buck with its long, twisted, beautifully annulated horns is perhaps the most arrestingly good-looking of all antelopes though only middle-sized. It is exclusively Indian and the fastest long-distance runner of all animals. The Chowsingha or Fourhorned Antelope is the only wild beast with four horns (a pair of knob-horns in front of a pair of spike-horns)—only the buck is horned. The chowsingha is uniquely Indian, as also is the pony-sized Nilgai, biggest of the country's antelopes, mainly inhabiting its north-west.

As said, India has more kinds of deer than any other country. Two, the superbly antlered Barasingha of Madhya Pradesh (now reviving from being dangerously depleted) and the closely related Swamp Deer of Uttar Pradesh and Assam, are solely Indian. The beautiful Chital, almost wholly Indian, is there in most parts of the country, and has established itself in new habitats into which it was introduced. The Hog Deer or Para is the poor relation of the chital and favours grasslands in places in the north and north-east. There is a race of the European Red Deer in Kashmir, the Hangul, now reviving from being reduced to rarity. The Thamin or Brow-antlered Deer, which is also there outside India, has its Manipur race (termed Sangai) alarmingly reduced to about a dozen animals, whose fate hangs in the balance. The Sambar, largest of Asiatic deer, has its largest population in India and attains its noblest bodily and antler development only here: it is a feature of most forests of the country. The Mouse Deer, only a little larger than a hare, and the widely distributed Muntjac or Barking Deer, along with the Himalayan Musk Deer, complete the tally of India's ten deer.

The Wild Boar is featured in the most ancient religious lore and legends of the country, and in an imperial emblem: it attains a most impressive size in places and a grown boar is such a formidable animal that even the tiger leaves it alone. Wild pig have a wide distribution all over India.

India's National Bird is the uniquely Indian Peacock. The peafowl of Sri Lanka were imported from India— peafowl have been exported from India even to Europe long, long ago. Other notable ground-birds include the Great Indian Bustard, floricans, and several kinds of partridges, quails and spurfowls. The Red Junglefowl of the northern half of the country is the ancestor of domestic poultry everywhere, and in the southern half is replaced by the 'Silverhackle', the Grey Junglefowl. A feature of the teeming avifauna of India is the vast numbers of migratory birds that sojourn here during winter. Notable among such migrants are the many kinds of ducks, many kinds of birds of prey (eagles, harriers

and the like), a host of plovers, sandpipers and warblers, and the Great White Crane from Siberia. In most parts of north India there is the no less magnificent native Sarus, the largest of all cranes.

The avifauna (comprising some 3000 species, of which nearly a third is not uncommon!) is so profuse that no proper account of it is possible in this survey. Luckily, there are excellent illustrated bird books that can be usefully consulted. The common indigenous water-birds breeding in spectacular nesting colonies may, however, be mentioned: the Grey Pelican, all 3 kinds of Indian cormorants and the Darter, the Grey and Purple Heron, the Night Heron and the Pond Heron, 3 kinds of true, snow-white egrets and the Cattle Egret, the White Ibis and the Spoonbill, the Painted Stork and the Openbilled Stork: the Little Grebe and the Indian Moorhen are usually to be found in the home water of mixed heronries.

15 Tiger Reserves, and around two dozen National Parks and 200 Sanctuaries constitute the preserves of the country's wildlife. However, this statistic gives no realistic idea of the position, for in many human activities are still permitted and some reserves are quite small. But it is true that national governmental awareness of the vital importance of conserving India's unique heritage of nature is more acute now, thanks mainly to the concern and realistic apprehension of Indira Gandhi, and that measures to safeguard the country's natural integrity are being devised and implemented. A live and vitally sustaining interest in a country's wildlife is such a natural human feeling in its citizens, but for centuries this interest has lain dormant in the vast majority of Indians. What is heartening is that today there are signs of the awakening of popular interest and pride in the manifold opulence of India's wildlife.

Cities of India

R.G.K.

It is not easy to write the history of Indian cities. There are *sthalapuranas,* local legends, relating to various places. We cannot rely on them though they are not to be dismissed as nonsense since they perhaps represent the psyche of a people. Like most other cities of the world the cities of India too—most of them at any rate—have grown haphazardly. But it is those cities that have grown organically that have a personality of their own. When you mention Leningrad or Paris, certain images are formed in your mind and certain immediate associations. These are cities that breathe, that are coloured by history. India too has such cities, many with ancient heritages.

The concept of a planned city is not new. Even as long ago as the time of the Harappan culture there were planned urban centres with neat streets, baths and arrangements for the disposal of garbage. Pataliputra, the ancient Magadhan capital (the name Patna is derived from it) was built according to a plan. Some years ago, a manuscript was discovered in Orissa in which there were instructions about how a city was to be built. The concept of a *nagarika* meaning both a city-dweller and a man with urbane qualities had developed in the early centuries and we find a reflection of this in Sanskrit drama, Tamil poetry and other texts. So much is mentioned to show that what is called the Indian civilization has had as much to do with urban life as with the soil and cultivation.

Some of the old cities of India have gone into oblivion; others have decayed. We know today little of Indraprastha or Hastinapur associated with the ancient Hindu epic, the *Mahabharata* or of cities of mythology built by architects like Maya possessing magical powers. Ayodhya of the other great epic, the *Ramayana,* is a sad relic of the past. Muziris on the Kerala coast had traded with West Asia, Greece and Rome and China in the dim past, so too Pumpuhar on the east coast. Today they survive only in name. The great Vijayanagar capital Hampi is in ruins and even the ruins have a splendour of their own. Bharuch on the Gujarat coast is today an unimportant town. The university cities of Taxila (Takshashila, now in Pakistan) and Nalanda remain only in the textbooks of history.

The so-called modern cities of India like Bombay, Calcutta and Madras still retain elements of Indianness and they still pulsate with life in spite of the industries that choke them. But it is to the smaller cities that we must turn, to experience India and its life. Let us look at four places Varanasi, Kanchipuram, Thanjavur and Mysore. They are hardly cities in the modern sense, like Bombay

Images on Varanasi walls.

and Calcutta or like Tokyo and Moscow. But they are cities with a history and the first three especially are of considerable antiquity. Together they represent India in many concrete and intangible ways.

Of the four cities Varanasi is the only one from the north of India. But because of its holiness it belongs not only to all of India but to the entire world. Varanasi, also called Kashi, is in Uttar Pradesh, India's most populous state. One of the world's oldest cities, it stands on the western bank of the river Ganga. But its geography is not important, nor its history. For it is a place in the hearts of Indians. For centuries from before the time of the Buddha it has represented the mind of India, the spirit of India. Ashoka, Chandragupta, Harshavardhana and perhaps the great Chola King who came to be called Gangaikondan must have come here. So too the Mughal Emperors Akbar, Jahangir and Aurangzeb. It has been a kind of open university of religious, philosophical and scientific disciplines bathed by the noble waters of the Ganga.

Now the Ganga is not only the river Ganga which rises in the Himalayas and, traversing the plains of the north, empties itself into the Bay of Bengal. There is also a Ganga of other worlds, a Ganga of the mind, a Ganga which is a pure concept. It is this stream that is eternal, the mother of all rivers. And to the devout in India any stream, any spring is like the Ganga. And so too Varanasi or Kashi. Kashi too is an idea, a "conceptualised" city of learning and of liberation. The idea of Kashi or the essence of Kashi, or its qualities, could be imparted to any city that we believe to be sacred or that we think is capable of helping us in our liberation.

Varanasi seems buried in the coils of Time, yet it has a presence that is immediate. It is of this world and beyond; and changing, it remains unchanged. That is why, like Rome, it is called the Eternal City. Varanasi is, however, not noted for its architectural splendour. The splendour is the city itself, for it is "Kashi", the city that glitters, the city that means light and illumines your heart and mind.

Varanasi is the city of Shiva, the Cosmic Lord, who is the Destroyer, but as Ishvara also grants grace and protection. Indeed he too is Creator and Sustainer. Shiva the Destroyer does not destroy man. He destroys the world of illusion. Indeed he destroys Death itself, destroys Time. For everything that is bound by Time must perish. By freeing the devout from Time he makes them timeless. Thus it is that people come to Kashi to die. To die without dying. That is to die and become part of the Timeless Truth. And that is the ultimate purpose of Varanasi, the city that is the end of man's pilgrimage, the city of fulfilment.

We will skip the history of the city. For history is measured by time and here is a city that dispenses timelessness to men and women suffering from the narrowness of time and space. Yet Kashi is not all about the cycle of birth and death. It exists on many levels. The city pulsates. The breath and sweat and longings of millions of people living in the city proclaim that it is very much of this world. The narrow claustrophobic streets echo to the cries and music of men and women who are very much involved in the struggles and temptations of existence. You find here the squalor and filth of Calcutta and Bombay. Yet Kashi has an indefinable quality that other cities lack. One would not like to call it Indianness. It is a universal mystique that cannot be described but has to be experienced. In the streets, in the bazar and in the bathing ghats you encounter men and women deeply engrossed in the present, in the struggle for existence, but their faces proclaim that they belong to an India that is centuries old. Kashi stands on

the Ganga but it also stands on the eternal stream of India and it represents the contradictions of India, its exaltation and its occasional lowliness.

You hear the cries of vendors, of the sellers of milk and curds. You may buy here bangles and vessels made of copper and brass and shining in the sun. The saris of Varanasi with their silver and gold are like the spires of its temples. And there are shops that sell little copper pots filled with the water of the Ganga, pots that are broken open and emptied into the mouths of dying men and women. Kashi the city of light, is the city of *moksha* or release, salvation. The bathing ghats come into view for a pilgrim boating on the river like a heavenly vision, a magnificent spectacle without any parallel. The ghats are alive all through the day with pilgrims from all over India. They echo to the chants of the Vedas, to music, to the prayers recited by the devout. Pandits sit under parasols and expound some story or some belief. Generation after generation of the devout have come here to bathe in the river and feel in its ripples the presence of all the great sages and thinkers of India. They offer libations to the departed, offer *pinda* or balls of rice to propitiate the *pitr*, all the ancestral spirits. They bring their own priests with them or are led away by avaricious vendors of salvation.

Above left : bathing ghats by the river at Varanasi. Above and left : worshippers and pilgrims make offerings in Varanasi.

But they do not mind being exploited. The idea of exploitation has no meaning in this eternal city which promises release from all bondage. Kashi is above all an experience: with all its worldliness, it is an experience of transcendence. Indeed the enticements of Kashi are part of the spiritual journey. And even the courtesans here have something to teach: the ephemeral nature of pleasure points out the futility of attachment.

Varanasi or Kashi is a complete Indian city, a three-faced city representing ancient, medieval and modern India. The seeker here receives illumination, perceptions of the Ultimate Reality. The story is told that during the great deluge when everything else will be destroyed, Kashi will remain as Light Eternal. It is one of the foremost of *tirthas*, a ford or crossing for mankind from the physical world to a new world of eternal life and bliss. For here in Varanasi, in Kashi, at the ford, the light reveals your own inner self.

From Varanasi in the north to Kanchipuram in the south it is hundreds of kilometres. Great distances do not pose a problem to the traveller and the pilgrim today when a journey across continents is undertaken in a few hours. But even in the old days, before the advent of the steam engine and the aeroplane, the devout were not deterred by great distances.

Now Kanchipuram is also one of the most sacred places of India. It is a place of great antiquity. "Nagareshu Kanchi", so goes a Sanskrit saying, which means Kanchipuram is the first city to be mentioned when we talk of cities, or the saying could mean Kanchi is *the* city The word Kanchi means a girdle and it is presumed the city is the centre of the girdle of the earth. In other words

Top : intricate carving at the entrance of the Kailasanatha Temple. Above : weavers at Kanchipuram. Opposite page : the soaring spire of the Brihadishvara Temple, Thanjavur.

Kanchipuram has a central place in the religious and cultural history of India. And at one time it had considerable political importance too. Today it is a district town in the state of Tamil Nadu and it is hardly two hours drive by road from Madras. Flowing west of the city is the river Palar.

The history of Kanchipuram could be traced from as early a period as the third century B.C. At one time many of the faiths of the land flourished here, Hinduism, Buddhism and Jainism. It was famous for its *ghatikas* where Vedic education was imparted. From the second or third century A.D. well into medieval times it was associated with some of the important names in Buddhism. Of them we will mention only one: Bodhidharma. He was reputedly born a prince in Kanchipuram (some others have it that he was born a Brahmin) and came to be known for his Dhyana school in Buddhism. He journeyed to China in those hazardous times (sixth century) and taught there. Dhyana came to be called Chan in China which was further transformed into Zen in Japan.

It is believed that Shankaracharya, the great Advaitic philosopher, founded one of his *mathas* here. A *matha* is an establishment particularly of *sannyasins*, those who have renounced the world to propagate their teaching. Thus the Kanchi Kamakoti Pitham is a celebrated attraction for seekers, particularly in south India, and they are firm in their belief that the Pitham or seat was founded by Adi Shankara (the first Shankara or Shankaracharya; successive heads of the *mathas* founded by him are also called Shankaracharyas). The present Shankaracharya of Kanchi, Shri Chandrasekharendra Sarasvati, is regarded as godlike by thousands of his devotees. He is indeed one of the most attractive figures of contemporary India with a presence that is compelling. The learned belonging to various countries come to him to be illumined. The Shankaracharya, who is in his nineties and is remarkably spry for his age, is extremely erudite and a storehouse of traditional knowledge and wisdom. Besides he has an extraordinary grasp of modern knowledge. We have said all this because

today the centuries-old city of Kanchi is more or less identified with him.

It would be interesting to speculate as to how Kanchipuram would have looked in ancient times. Here men of adventure, men seeking wisdom or a fortune must have come from as far away as China, West Asia, Greece and Rome. Debates must have been held on various systems of religion and philosophy and the merchandise from many parts of the world must have found its way here. Kanchipuram has more temples than any other place. They are almost a hundred in number.

Kanchipuram has known many dynasties. The Pallavas probably established their rule in these parts in the early centuries of the Christian era. The Kadambas and the Gangas from the Karnataka region, the Cholas and the Rashtrakutas have held sway here. The Chalukyas and the Hoysalas too have been associated with Kanchipuram. Among the best remembered dynasties we must mention the Pallavas. They are known to the world as the builders of those marvellous rock-cut temples on the east coast, not far from Madras: we are referring to Mamallapuram or Mahabalipuram. Indeed the foundation of the Dravidian style of architecture was laid by the Pallavas. In Kanchipuram itself there are two famous temples built by the Pallavas: Kailasanatha and Vaikunthaperumal, both belonging to the eighth century. They are both noted for their elegance and the exuberance of the later Dravidian style is not foreshadowed by them.

Both the Vaishanava temple to Varadarajasvami and the Shaiva temple to Ekamreshvara (Lord of One Mango) are magnificent places of worship, imposing, lofty and extensive in their construction. It appears Krishnadevaraya (16th century, Vijayanagar Empire) visited both these temples and some believe that the division of the city into Vishnu Kanchi and Shiva Kanchi owed to him. The temple to Kamakshi is believed to have associations with Shankara who installed a *chakra* in the sanctum. (The *chakra* is part of the Shakta ritual of the worship of Devi regarded as the Supreme Deity).

Many of the great temples of Kanchi are in a state of disrepair. But in our imagination we can recall the splendour in ancient and medieval times when poets and pilgrims and merchants and philosophers must have come to the city on foot or in palanquins. Today Kanchipuram is also famous for its handloom fabrics, particularly silk saris. These are the ultimate in fashion to Indian women and are unrivalled for their varied colours and gorgeousness.

Shaiva and Vaishnava saint-poets have sung here. Naturally such a place as this must have drawn many musicians of the Karnatak school (which is different from the Hindustani school of the north). In spite of its apparent decay the visitor would be persuaded to believe that once upon a time Kanchipuram must have had the glitter of what it was supposed to be—the girdle of the earth.

Thanjavur, further south and again in Tamil Nadu (it is about 350 kilometres from Madras), is quintessentially South India or, at any rate, quintessentially Tamil. (Tanjore was the anglicised name of the city as well as of the district of that name. The present official spelling is Thanjavur. Though the name has an "h", it is not aspirated when you pronounce it). The district of Thanjavur lies in the lap of the sacred river Kaveri, in fact in its delta. It is fertile and lush and is the rice bowl of Tamil Nadu. Centuries ago the great Chola kings built an earthern dam, called the Grand Anicut, which still feeds the network of irrigation canals in the area. Around Thanjavur city lie a number of places of great cultural interest. Thiruvaiyaru is one such and here were born in the 18th century three of the

greatest composers of Karnatak music—Shyamashastri, Tyagaraja and Muttusvami Dikshitar. Tyagaraja spent most of his life in Thiruvaiyaru, on the banks of the Kaveri and his memorial or *samadhi* is here. His death anniversary is celebrated every year with performances of music, a great music festival. The festival usually falls in January and those who wish to take part in it usually stay in Thanjavur and visit Thiruvaiyaru every day by bus or car.

It is claimed music and dance came naturally to people in Thanjavur, also mathematics. Once upon a time there lived in the city prosperous landowners who had the leisure to cultivate the arts. They spent their time discussing the finer points of a *raga* (mode or melody in Indian music) or listening to vocal and instrumental recitals. One of the instruments for which the place has been famous is the majestic pipe called the *nagasvaram*, a wonderful processional instrument used at weddings and temple rituals. Thanjavur is the home of that great style of classical dance called Bharata Natyam.

A large percentage of Indian coffee is grown in Karnataka. But it must have been in Tamil Nadu, particularly Thanjavur, that South Indian coffee must have evolved. This coffee is unlike any other coffee in the world and it has a unique flavour, a flavour that is as civilised as the Chola bronzes. Popularly known as "filter coffee" it is not the colour of coffee but that of sandal-paste. It is made of the finest beans, roasted lovingly and ground to proper grainy consistency. The "decoction" is made by pouring boiling water over the powder kept in a vessel with a perforated bottom. You need fresh milk to make the coffee unforgettably delicious.

Thanjavur has got its character through centuries of Chola rule. It has also come under the Vijayanagar Empire and later under the Nayaks who broke off from the Vijayanagar Empire. Subsequently came the Marathas and the British. The arts flourished under all these regimes. Chola bronzes are famous all over the world and they are perhaps unsurpassed in Indian metal sculpture. Some of these bronzes are kept in the Sarasvati Mahal of Thanjavur. The Marathas patronised music and dance. It is likely Bharata Natyam as it is known today was perfected by a family called the "Thanjavur quartet" though this theory has been disputed by some historians of dance.

Thanjavur is famous for its lanes and by-lanes, for its restaurants where you get not only good coffee but those south Indian delicacies, *iddalis* and *dosas*, which are now popular all over India. We don't know who made the first *iddalis* and *dosas*, but here in Thanjavur they are like nowhere else. There are people skilled in the making of musical instruments here and also in metalware.

The most famous attraction in Thanjavur is the Brihadishvara temple. It is a sanctuary to the great god Shiva and was built by the Chola Emperor Rajaraja the Great (10th-11th centuries). It is an unimaginably splendid structure as if it were built to proclaim the glory of India, the glory of Shiva seated on the mountain Kailasa. Its gopuram or tower is 68 metres high and the walled enclosure is 152 metres by 76 metres. The engineering skill of the builders of this temple is demonstrated in the towered sanctuary or *vimana* which takes off in a vertical manner from its square base for 15 metres and then tapers off until the whole structure attains a height of 58 metres. There are beautiful carvings. Altogether the impression made by the temple is that of artistic grandeur of which the only parallel is the incomplete temple, also a Chola monument, at Gangaikondacholapuram.

From Thanjavur to Mysore City. The term Mysore

Top : street scene Thanjavur. Above : the middle gopuram or tower of the Brihadishvara Temple, Thanjavur. Opposite page : worshippers at a temple, Thanjavur.

Summer palace of Tipu Sultan at Srirangapattana, near Mysore.

City is used to distinguish it from the former princely state of Mysore which now forms part of the larger entity, Karnataka. Mysore shares with Thanjavur certain qualities that are distinctively south Indian. Until independence it represented the pageantry of princely rule because the Maharaja of Mysore lived in his splendid palace here. And the Maharaja of Mysore along with those of Travancore and Cochin in the south belonged to a special category. They were all enlightened rulers who took their states to the forefront of their country.

Mysore City thus has always been considered a city of courtiers, musicians and scholars. One cannot, though, speak of the courtiers now. But something of the old courtesies still remain. Perhaps you still see in this graceful city stately men with gold-bordered turbans and picturesque and gentle women. One remembers going through the serene streets of the residential area of Mysore and greeted by the melodies of the *vina* played perhaps by some beautiful young woman to the goddess Chamundeshvari, the presiding deity of Mysore. The imposing palaces here are set off by blocks of small new houses and the university campus with its poetic name, "Manasagangotri" meaning the spring or source of the Ganga of the mind. The man who thought up the name: K.V. Puttappa or Kuvempu, as he is affectionately called, one of the great figures in contemporary Kannada poetry.

There is nothing of the harshness of metropolitan cities here, nothing of the aggressiveness of modern life. Mysore is tucked away, so to speak, in southern parts of Karnataka. It is reminiscent of the fictional place Malgudi created by the writer R.K. Narayan in his short and long stories of humour and irony, stories that say so much in a simple and direct manner. Mysore is like Malgudi because it is more than what it appears to be, more than what it would speak to you were it able to give voice to its own character.

As with many other cities of India, especially of the south, Mysore too has changed hands during the centuries. There is a story that Chandragupta Maurya, the great imperial monarch of the north, travelled to Sravanabelagola in 301 B.C. to become a Jain monk. This place is not far from Mysore. The Chalukyas, the Rashtrakutas, the Vijayanagar kings, the Hoysalas must have ruled Mysore. It has been in the hands of Hyder Ali and his son Tipu Sultan, one of the great warriors and generals India has produced during the past few centuries. He died in 1799 at Srirangapattana, also near Mysore, heroically fighting the British. The Wadiyars have ruled Mysore since the 17th century up to the time India became free except for the years during which the kingdom of Mysore was held by Hyder Ali and Tipu Sultan. They were patrons of the arts and they encouraged musicians from all parts of India.

The city of Mysore is overlooked by the Chamundi Hill, about a thousand metres above sea-level. Chamundi is the name of the tutelary diety of the Wadiyars. Up on the hill, before you reach the summit, is a colossal figure of a Nandi, the sacred bull of Shiva, carved out of the basalt of the hill. The Maharaja's Palace is Indo-Saracenic in design with Hoysala carvings. Its Durbar Hall brings to mind the fabulous wealth of the princely rulers. According to one account the throne was presented to Chikkadeva Raja of Mysore by the Mughal Emperor

Above : Brindavan Gardens, near Mysore, lit up at night.
Opposite page right : a traditional couple from Mysore.
Right : interior of the palace at Mysore. Far right :
Mysore : city of music. Rapt audience at a concert in the
main hall of the palace.

Aurangzeb late in the 17th century. Another palace, the Lalita Mahal, was used to house distinguished guests. The Jaganmohan Palace is another stately mansion.

Those visiting Mysore do not usually fail to go to the nearby town of Srirangapattana and the Krishnarajasagar Dam. Srirangapattanam, nine miles from Mysore City, is renowned as a Vaishnava centre and is of historic importance. The Ranganathasvami temple is in the Dravidian style of architecture and has a fine gopuram. The deity, Ranganathasvami (Lord of the Stage), is Vishnu reclining on the great snake Shesha and the image is awe-inspiring in its dimensions.

The fortress here was built in the 15th century. East of this is the Darya Daulat Bagh, the summer palace of Tipu Sultan, on the Kaveri. Srirangapattana itself is an island on the Kaveri and its water supply was provided by means of an ingenious aqueduct constructed by Tipu Sultan. The Krishnarajasagar Dam is about two miles from Srirangapattana. Krishnarajasagar is a marvellous lake and leading to it is the famous Brindavan Gardens, a popular tourist attraction.

The small towns in India are becoming big towns and the big towns are becoming cities. Since independence urbanisation has been going on at a rapid pace. Much of the charm of places like Mysore is because of gardens and a sense of space and serenity. Other places, especially in the south, are famous for their temples. Chidambaram, for example. Or Madurai. Trivandrum and Hyderabad are state capitals and still their identity has not been erased by industrial expansion.

India is not all Delhi, Bombay, Calcutta and Madras. Perhaps it is difficult to discover all the faces of India. It is an endless quest and a beautifully rewarding experience, discovering India in its many towns and cities, India changing, yet retaining that indefinable quality that cannot be changed.

Indian theatre – in search of identity

RATAN THIYAM

Over the last decade, Indian theatre has arrived on the international theatre scene with a distinct identity of its own. Plays like "Ghashiram Kotwal" performed by the Theatre Academy of Pune, and Habib Tanvir's "Charandas Chor", have been viewed outside India, and the latest success is that of the Chorus Repertory Theatre from Imphal in Manipur with "Chakravyuha". "Chakravyuha", after delighting audiences in the Soviet Union, went on to win an award at the Edinburgh Festival and played in London and Dublin as well.

These plays, as indeed many others now being staged in India, have different themes and languages. But they all have an element in common: they are questing, experimental. The nature of experiment in contemporary Indian theatre is multi-dimensional. It is a kind of synthesis between modern techniques and stagecraft on the one hand and ancient Indian traditions on the other; and the combination has given a forceful thrust to contemporary theatrical expression. Indian theatre has a unique heritage of innumerable traditional art forms, whose codification has

Above : war and its grim aftermath are powerfully portrayed in the play "Andha Yug". Right : the Queen accuses the thief in Habib Tanvir's play "Charandas Chor" which uses folk tunes and techniques.

Top : The ritual form of Theyyam used to dramatic effect in "Urubhangam", a tragedy based on an episode from the epic the Mahabharata. The same epic also provides the content for the play "Chakravyuha", a scene from which is seen at the right.

ensured their continuity and which have been performed for over three thousand years. Indian theatre is Total Theatre in the real sense, amply fulfilling the definition of theatre as a composite art form.

The roots of the Indian theatrical tradition lie in the massive and ancient treatise, the *Natya Shastra*, ascribed to the sage Bharata and to a period in the centuries immediately preceding the Christian era. The *Natya Shastra* is a compilation of practices and beliefs concerning the performing arts. This remarkably comprehensive volume dealt with the stage, dance, drama, music, elocution; it detailed techniques, movements and gestures, and described the stage, theatre architecture, make-up, and costume. It spoke about both spiritual depth and the height of aesthetics of a performance, even analysing the literary nuances of a text. It was important that the spec-

tator participated by being responsive; thus, the sentiments of both performer and spectator are described. The *Natya Shastra* has been like a powerful encyclopaedia of theatre art, a source of inspiration for directors, playwrights, actors, dancers, musicians and designers. Bharata's detailed descriptions of sentiments and emotions—whose hues and shades he has faithfully documented after what appears to be a clinical and scientific study—are as valid today as they ever were. The relevance of the *Natya Shastra* has not faded with time, and it is still the companion of modern experimentalists in the contemporary theatre scene.

There were other equally well-documented treatises on various aspects of the Art; Nandikeshwar's *Abhinaya Darpana* and Abhinava Gupta's *Abhinav Bharati*, and Dhananjay's *Dasa Roopaka* are some of the well known books. They have contributed to enhance the knowledge of performance theory to a great extent. Their teachings are still as fresh and clean as they were when written for the first time, and their theories have stood the test of time.

Classical Indian theatre had Sanskrit as its language of expression, and was supported by the patronage of the courts, thus giving it a somewhat aristocratic flavour. Around the 10th century A.D. the continuity of the tradition was disrupted by socio-political circumstances, and the evolution of modern languages. The tradition, in a fragmented form, continued in various regions of India, giving rise to a regional theatre identity influenced by local conditions of geography and politics. There was then a gradual incorporation of folk traditions into the classical framework, an enrichment which not only made the form more accessible to the people whose language was now being used for theatrical expression, but also gave it a local idiom and meaning.

A similar movement toward the grass roots was taking place in other fields. Ideas which were once confined to the elite were brought to the people in their masses through the use of simpler local language and symbols that were easily accessible. The wisdom of the Hindu scriptures, the Vedas and Upanishads, were thus spread and disseminated to the people; and a similar process repeated itself in literature, where regional languages started gaining in importance.

Through the middle ages, the classical tradition lingered on in the regional folk forms; even now, we glimpse it in the folk forms of various parts of the country. With the arrival of the British in India, the scene changed yet again. The elite of the country were offered an alternative to the classical tradition, for the British brought with them the form of the Elizabethan theatre both through professional companies and amateur groups. Those among the Indians who came into contact with these foreigners and who learned their language were exposed to the rich theatrical traditions of Shakespeare and the other European masters. They started translating or adapting Shakespeare into vernacular or regional languages. Some of them did try to write Indian stories, but the impact and the influence of the West was visible in their writings. One could find a Macbeth or a Shylock in Indian garb in these plays. This kind of theatre was exemplified by the Parsi Theatre tradition, which used easy-to-understand and colloquial Hindustani as its language of expression, and was popular all over the country until the advent of the spoken cinema, the talkies, in the nineteen thirties.

The influence of the West had a strong grip over the style of presentation in Indian theatre. But the contents and the themes of drama changed, particularly with the

Top : the duel between brain and brawn : scene from "Hayavadana". Above : scene from "Barnam Vana", a Hindi verse translation of Shakespeare's "Macbeth". Opposite page : the Peshwa, his bride and the police chief in a compelling moment from the brilliant production "Ghashiram Kotwal".

strong movement towards freedom. Many plays were written against political oppression and dominance, or showing the Indian aspiration for freedom. The pre-independence decade of the late thirties and early forties saw the rejuvenation of the theatrical tradition which had been started by Bharatendu Harishchandra in Hindi, Rabindra Nath Tagore in Bengali and the Kirloskars in Marathi. The political turmoil in the thirties, the great famine and the Second World War, started a unique movement of theatre which, on the one hand, tried to present the harsh realities of life, and on the other, tried to discover an Indian idiom of theatrical expression. Playwrights like Bijon Bhattacharya and directors like Sombhu Mitra spearheaded this movement through the Central Squad of the Indian Peoples Theatre Association. This concern for the present, for the social realities of today, is very much a hallmark of contemporary Indian theatre, which is replete with themes based on social relevance and the voice of protest. Tales from mythology or folk lore are used as allegories to convey the people's mood, a feeling, or attitude.

When freedom came to India, it liberated our theatre from the shackles of Western models and from the mindless borrowing from these models. Indian theatre embarked on a journey of rediscovery of its glorious classical traditions, which had sustained themselves through the centuries in folk forms. Folk and traditional forms integrated dance and music with the dramatic form; dance and music were natural corollaries of the theatrical expression, making it into a composite whole. The folk forms had been shorn of the codified rigidity of the classical tradition, and had gained many strong elements such as spontaneity, exuberance and flexibility.

The movement towards social realism caught on and become popular with theatre workers all over the country. The fifties and the sixties became the decades of self-awareness of the Indian theatre. Classical texts were re-discovered and re-interpreted to make them relevant to contemporary situations. Codified treatises on dramaturgy were studied in detail to determine the exact nature of the classical format and the possibility of its adaptation to the contemporary scene. Playwrights wrote in the local idiom: not just the language, but also using the folk and classical traditions of their regions. The results were very encouraging, and led to works where the strength of the content was matched by spontaneity and vitality of presentation. In short, a whole new theatre movement, uniquely Indian, was flourishing in several languages, led by fine playwrights such as Mohan Rakesh, Vijay Tendulkar and Girish Karnad.

Girish Karnad's "Hayavadana" is based on a story from an ancient Sanskrit anthology, the *Kathasaritsagar*. The play drew on the Yakshagana tradition of Karnataka as well as folk forms to tell its story of transposed heads. The head of a cultured and learned man is accidentally grafted to the body of a man of superb physique and strength but limited mental capacity, and vice versa. Based on an ancient theme, using ancient conventions such as the *bhagavata* or narrator who is the link between various episodes, Karnad's play raises some contemporary issues of human incompleteness, of fractured identities.

Vijay Tendulkar used *Khel, Tamasha* and other western Indian traditional forms in his brilliant and biting "Ghashiram Kotwal", which was directed by Jabbar Patel. Set in a period of Maratha history before the advent of the British, the play is about a society corrupted by excesses, intrigues and superstition. Most of all, the play is about power—and what it does to people—told

the episode of an impenetrable military formation and the slaying of the brave young warrior, Abhimanyu. The play evolved in a workshop and was scripted in a manner that involved the actor's confrontation with different aspects of the science of theatre—in which the actor is, at one time, observer, participant and performer. "Chakravyuha" raises questions through its presentation of the central character of Abhimanyu. Was he a martyr, a scapegoat of a treacherous system, or a sacrificial offering in the great battle for power?

Experimentation with plays from other countries has led to some interesting offerings on the contemporary stage. B.V. Karanth's production of "Barnam Vana", a Hindi verse translation of Shakespeare's "Macbeth" by noted poet Raghuvir Sahay, used the fluid rhythm and dramatic style of Yakshagana, a form from Karanth's home state of Karnataka. In a note, Karanth commented on his use of this form, and wrote: "The tragedies of Shakespeare, especially "Macbeth", overflow with *rasas* (emotions) such as valour, wrath, terror or wonder, and the characters and situations have a universality and larger-than-life quality which can be well expressed in the Yakshagana style. This form is specially developed in its presentation of characters' entries and exits, battle scenes, and the expression of emotional tensions through the rhythm of body movements." In his production, Karanth used costumes based on traditional theatre costumes from Japan, Bali, Burma and Indonesia, and introduced Asian musical instruments such as gongs and bells. It all added up, as Karanth put it, to a search for "new dimensions in the theatrical experience", an encounter in text and form where east met west.

This search has been extended in the productions of talented directors and producers such as Vijaya Mehta, Jabbar Patel and B.M. Shah, among others, all of whom have created their own style and are outstanding figures of contemporary Indian theatre.

The movement of re-discovery and adaptation is gaining strength every day with increasing numbers of theatre workers who want to study folk and traditional forms and adapt them for the contemporary situation. This movement has thrown up many serious directors like Bhanu Bharati, Kanhailal, Bansi Kaul, Muthuswamy, Sankhya Ibotombi, S. Ramanujam, a movement which covers the whole nation. All these figures are trying to evolve a style of presentation which is unique in its Indian-ness.

It is also fascinating to note that contemporary South East Asian theatre, and particularly modern Japanese theatre, are also trying to experiment with their traditions as a language of expression, using many theatre performing arts forms. One recalls especially Noh, which is a product of Tseami's *Kedensho*, the six hundred years old treatise of spiritual enlightenment of an actor aiming for *Hana*. It is indeed an interaction between traditional performing arts and modern theatre. And still applicable in this highly industralised and technological age, because the primary concern of both Tseami and Bharata muni was the art of an actor.

The art of the actor is the process of communication; and this is what contemporary theatre in India seeks to do. Through its many languages, expressing local forms and idioms, our theatre both explores its roots and thrusts in new directions. Supported by the activities of the National School of Drama, with its unique theatre training programme, and by many enthusiastic drama groups across the country, contemporary theatre is alive with vigour and spontaneity.

through the rise and fall of the police chief, Ghashiram. The play used the device of a human wall—a convention of the Konkan folk form, the *Khel*—in a brilliant and versatile manner. The movements of this human wall were choreographed so that its members sometimes froze to become flowers and trees in a garden, or were transformed into a wedding procession, or became a frenzied mob, or quite simply turned their backs on the audience like a row of blank, shut doors. The innovative use of a wide variety of musical styles, the twisting plot, the satirical dialogue, made this a memorable theatre event with a contemporary edge. Mani Madhukar's "Rasa Gandharva" and some of his other plays used the Khayal form with good effect.

Habib Tanvir, a noted director of Hindi theatre, turned to the folk tunes and techniques of the Chhatisgarh area of central India to present Hindi versions of Sanskrit classics. One of his best-known attempts is "Charandas Chor", an authentic dialect play whose contemporary theme is presented by a folk group cast. Using another region, and another group of forms, Kavalam Narayan Panikkar turned to his native state of Kerala in south India and used Kathakali, Theyyam and Koodiyattam to reinforce his themes. Koodiyattam is considered to be the form nearest to the classical traditions of ancient Sanskrit drama. In his version of "Urubhangam", based on the play by the classical Sanskrit playwright, Bhasa, Panikkar used Theyyam, the traditional ritualistic dance of Kerala. "Urubhangam" is a tragedy based on an episode from the great epic, the *Mahabharata*, and though set in an ancient period, forcefully brings home a message relevant to our times—that of the futility of war. The supernatural dimensions of Theyyam with its elaborate masks and stately movements added to the production of "Urubhangam".

Another modern presentation of an episode from the *Mahabharata* has been done by the writer of this article using the powerful motifs of theatrical expression that enrich the traditional and folk forms of Manipur in the north east of India. Manipur's martial arts and other forms such as Warileeba, Nata Sankirtana, and Cholom, were woven into the fabric of "Chakravyuha", based on

Himalayan art

MADANJEET SINGH

The Himalaya, meaning the "abodes of snow", are the world's tallest mountain ranges whose spiny ridges spread out half-way across the world's largest continent. These formidable mountains, comprising the highest summit in the world, Mount Everest (8848 mts), and some 30 peaks rising to 7300 mts., present an awe-inspiring spectacle that transcends description. Their soaring heights of snow-capped silvery peaks reach out beyond the horizon in a vast landscape of gigantic glaciers called *Himadri* or the Greater Himalaya; the brown, barren and rugged high plateau of *Himachal* or the Middle Himalaya; and the lush green forests and vegetation on the slopes of lower Himalaya called *Shiwalik* in the West and *Duars* in the East.

The Buddhist monasteries and Hindu temples are mostly situated in the Middle and Lower ranges of the Himalaya that are contained between the great bend of the river Indus in Kashmir in the west and the similar sharp turn of the river Brahmaputra in Upper Assam in the east; in between are 17 other rivers. Most of the Himalayan rivers flow in troughs, the trends of which are

Above : Lachung Monastery, Sikkim.
Above right : face of the Buddha from the Tawang Monastery, Arunachal Pradesh.

Above : image of the Buddha from Simtokha Monastery, Bhutan.
Opposite page : shrine at Alchi.

determined by the branching ranges of the Greater Himalaya.

It is at the intersections of the rivers that Himalayan shrines were traditionally built. They were located mostly in the vicinity of the major trade routes so that the lay devotees, mainly traders and merchants, could break their tedious and perilous journeys across the mountains. In return, the monasteries received donations from the guests. Based as they were on a popular culture and the community life of the people, these *Viharas* were largely self-supporting.

Himalayan art, as that of all India, owes its origin jointly to the Indus Valley civilization, which flourished between 2800 B.C.-1350 B.C., and the semi-nomadic Indo-Aryans, who in about 2500 B.C., were the first of the many immigrants into India. In praise and honour of the benign and destructive powers of nature, the Aryans composed hymns called the *Vedas* (divine knowledge), and as they descended into the Indus Valley, they probably assigned to the different elements, the forms of art objects created by that civilization. Among the few miniature sculptures in bronze, stone and terra-cotta which the newcomers found in Indus Valley, there are also the stone stamp seals and the relief steatite sealings struck from them. Some significant cult scenes or symbols include the tree spirit with a tiger standing before it; a horned tree spirit confronted by a worshipper; a composite beast with seven figures; and most interesting of them all, a horned deity seated in a yogic (meditative) posture and surrounded by all kinds of beasts. It is assumed that this deity was later associated with the Hindu god Shiva.

During the predominance of the Theravada form of Buddhism, the earliest examples in India of Buddhist art are the 2nd-1st century B.C. relief sculptures at Bharhut and Sanchi, in which the Buddha presence was indicated by symbols such as a throne, footprints, the Bo tree under which Gautama the Buddha achieved enlightenment and the *stupa*, symbolizing his final deliverance or death (in about 480 B.C.). Among the most outstanding works of art created under Emperor Ashoka's patronage (about 273-232 B.C.) were also the inscribed pillars which he erected in his extensive empire to spread the message of the Buddha. This motif, representing Himalaya as a world pillar supporting the *dharma-chakra* or the "wheel of law", also symbolizes Mount Kailasha near the sacred lake Manasarovara, which both Hindu cosmography and Buddhist pilgrim lore regard as the holiest of all places of pilgrimage. In the Himalayan region too several literary references and representations in art attest to the worship of these symbols, as for example the famous Ashoka pillars at Lumbini, Nigalisagar and Kundan in Nepal.

However it was not until the brief Kushan interlude of power in northwest India (50 B.C.-210 A.D.) that under their patronage the images of the Buddha in human form were made for the first time in Mathura and the region which was then called Gandhara (northwest Pakistan and eastern Afghanistan). The Mathura images were based on prototypes of an Indian *Yaksha* (nature deity), while the Gandhara sculptures were inspired by the Greco-Roman models. The interaction of these two styles on each other then developed into the classical sculptures of the Buddha image during the Gupta period. In these images the hand gestures (*mudras*) are indicative of important episodes in the life of the Buddha, the most popular being the preaching of the law; reassurance; the calling of the earth to witness; meditation; and the alms-bestowing attitude. In Himalayan sculptures and paintings such stylized images of the Buddha are seen side by side with narrative scenes of the

Top : painted panel from the Monastery at Likir.
Above : portable chapel, Tashigomang.

major events in his life.

Buddhist art continued to flourish under the patronage of the Guptas (320-530 A.D.), even though the rulers themselves venerated Vishnu. This Hindu god was depicted either sitting on his vehicle Garuda, the sun eagle; sleeping on the serpent Ananta; or in his incarnation as Krishna, the flute-playing cowherd, whose love for the milkmaid Radha is among the most popular themes in painting. But during their later period (530-770 A.D.) the Gupta pantheon incorporated new protector gods. During those difficult years of wars and conflict, help was also sought from Shiva, the lord of the mountain; Shiva now appeared in his more fierce aspect as Bhairava, (the terrible destroyer), while his consort Parvati, the erstwhile fair and peaceful daughter of the Himalaya, is now depicted as the awe inspiring Durga Mahishamardini, (slayer of the bull demon). It was during this period that the Buddha also was incorporated in the Hindu pantheon as one of Vishnu's incarnations.

Most early monuments in the Himalaya were made of wood and other perishable materials and have consequently disappeared, leaving us few examples of art in the region; surviving specimens are the ones in stone such as the Ashoka's incribed pillars, *stupas* and the Gupta inspired sculptures in Nepal valley and some exquisite Gandhara style images found in the Kashmir valley. In any case, Himalayan art remained confined to the lower reaches of the mountains until about the 7th century A.D. when Buddhism came to be recognized in Tibet in a form which was a synthesis of Mahayana and Vajrayana thought. Tradition has it that Buddhist art was introduced to Tibet by the daughter of king Amshuvarman of Nepal, who carried a sandalwood image of the Buddha when she married the Tibetan ruler Srongtsen-gampo (620-649 A.D.?). This seems to have opened up an exciting period in Himalayan art history, specially after the first

Tibetan monastery was build in Samye. This was followed by the arrival of the celebrated Tantric master Padmasambhava from India during the second half of the 8th century A.D. He is credited with having subdued the Bon spirits and demons by teaching the Tantrayogacharya doctrine. Contemporaneous with Padmasambhava was another Indian monk Shantirakshita and his disciple Kamalashila, who are said to have carried a number of Buddhist manuscripts as well as models of icons for the benefit of the devotees in the Himalayan regions.

Major monasteries in the Himalaya still possess a large number of manuscripts of both Mahayana and Vajrayana literature which formed the philosophical basis of the religion, and many of which are illustrated, containing elaborate instructions for making of the images. *Mahaprajnaparamita, Lankavatara, Saddharmapundarka, Sukhavati-vyuha* are among the Vajrayana treatises which inspired its different sects, while *Guhyasamaja, Manjushrimulakalpa, Sadhanamala, Nishpannayogavali*, are the most elaborate and vividly pictorial Tantric scriptures. Names of such great Indian pundits as Nagarjuna (2nd or 3rd century A.D.) Asanga, Vasubandhu (5th century A.D.), Sthiramati (6th century A.D.) are all associated with these manuscripts, which are said to have been originally obtained from the great monastic institutions in the Gangetic plains. The well known Mahaviharas at Bodhgaya, Nalanda, Odantapuri and Vikramashila served not only as theological schools but also contained scriptoria for illustrations and copying of manuscripts, as well as workshops for stone cutting and casting of bronzes.

The progressively complex and conventional forms of Buddhist medieval art proliferated in the Himalaya (770-1200). The pantheon rapidly expanded specially with the establishment of the five-fold celestial or Dhyani-Buddhas and their respective representations with two Bodhisattvas each.

According to an old Buddhist doctrine, the Bodhisattva is a wise and compassionate being who will ultimately become a Buddha. But his aim is to assist other living beings in their struggle for perfection; thus, even though he is destined to become a Buddha, he will wait until the humblest worshipper has reached the highest goal. Chief among the Bodhisattvas is Avalokiteshvara, "The Lord who looks down", whose special attribute is deep compassion for suffering humanity, and whose hand holds a lotus, symbol of perfection and knowledge. He is the earthly manifestation of the Buddha who presides over the highest heaven. Manjushri is the Bodhisattva of wisdom, usually depicted with a sword in one hand to destroy error and falsehood, and a book in the other. Manjushri and the compassionate Avalokiteshvara were particularly popular, and to them was added a whole series of deities, each distinguished by his or her own specific attributes. Such associated "families" of the Bodhisattvas included feminine consorts, Taras, as well as pacific and horrific aspects of the various divinities. For example the terrifying aspect of Manjushri is the fierce Vajrabhairava or Yamantaka, a nine-headed heavily armed deity who is depicted in a locked embrace with his consort while trampling on various creatures underfoot. Such occult concepts of Vajrayana not only transformed the simple cult images of the ascetic Buddha of earlier times into bejewelled and crowned Buddhas, but also caused the Buddha images to be vastly outnumbered by hundreds of gods and goddesses, many of whom were of Hindu origin. The unrelenting process of deification turned numerous objects, animals and even abstract con-

Above : small stupa shrine.

Above : Lamayuru Monastery, Ladakh.
Right : Buddhist images on stone, as seen all over Ladakh.

cepts into symbols of gods and goddesses. The five celestial Buddhas represent not only the centre and four compass points but also the Five Great Elements and the Five Components (material quality, feeling, perception, understanding and consciousness). Additionally, they warn against the Five Great Evils (ignorance, wrath, desire, malice and envy).

As in Hindu Tantric practices, Vajrayana devotees invoked deities who were described iconographically in Tantra scriptures. Holding the magic instrument *vajra*, a diamond or thunderbolt, the devotee summoned the presence of divinities with the help of *mudras*, *mantras* (magical syllables), and icons portraying a *mandala*. The *mandala* is a psychocosmogram in which the essence of a Tantric text is represented by syllables or visual symbols. This "ornament of the Buddha-mind", representing the universe and meant as an aid to mystical vision, thus became one of Buddhist art's most important themes, generally painted on cloth. A variation of the *mandala* is the Wheel of Existence which graphically depicts the Buddhist (and Hindu) view of life, in which time moves in cycles (*kalapas*). Its concentric circles and sections symbolize the plurality of the Universe, and its revolving cycles of periods of destruction and re-creation. In its Tantric interpretation, it is depicted in the shape of a circle which Mara, the lord of death, holds in his teeth and in between his arms and legs. Round the edge of the circle are twelve small inset pictures representing the twelve-fold causal nexus binding living beings to the sorrows of the inner circle.

The duality of the sexes was developed with particular emphasis during Tantric ascendency in both Hindu and Buddhist religions. *Dhyana*, or meditation as abstract thought, was regarded as the male principle which remained inert until activated by a cosmic female energy, *shakti;* in Buddhist Tantra, the female component is an appreciative awareness, *prajna*, and not the power *shakti* of Hinduism. Its hundreds of variations are seen in Himalayan shrines where the Hindus have their eternal divine couples Shiva-Parvati, Vishnu-Lakshmi, et cetera. The Buddhist display their yab-yum (father-mother) couples in forms such as Heruka with his Prajna: Heruka is the fierce form of the celestial Buddha Akshobaya, which appears to have been adopted by Tantric Buddhists from the fierce form of the Hindu god Shiva.

Stylistically too, medieval Himalayan art had come a long way since the Indus Valley settlers adopted the image of the Shiva-prototype, the divine yogi of the Himalaya. Based on the art forms which developed successively under the patronages of the Mauryan, Kushan and Gupta dynasties, its art forms now blossomed in varied styles of regional schools, which in turn drew on the cultures of the Karkotas in Kashmir, the Gurjara-Pratiharas in central Himalaya, the Pala-Sena in Nepal and on Tibet's artistic genius. By this time such peripheral influences as those of central Asia could also be distinguished in the western Himalaya, reflecting the rather confusing welter of cultures in the Tarim Basin which was at the time the crucible of such beliefs as Shamanism, Zoroastrianism, Nestorian Christianity and finally Islam. As the art of Gandhara aided the missionary expansion of Buddhism in central Asia, some of the Mahayana Bodhisattvas such as Manjushri, Amitabha and Avalokiteshvara may well have been inspired in part under Zoroastrian influences. There is evidence too of some degree of syncretism between Buddhism and Manichaeism, an Iranian dualistic religion that was founded in the 3rd century A.D. Similarly, Chinese in-

Above : images from Phyang.
Opposite page : painting of Avalokitesvara from Sinon Monastery in Sikkim.

fluences in art seem to have come via Kucha, Khotan, Karashahr, Turfan, Aksu and so on. Even after the decline of these states, Buddhism continued to flourish until about the 11th century A.D. under the patronage of the Uighur Turks. Examples of this kind of hybrid art can still be seen in the beautiful paintings in monasteries such as Alchi in Ladakh (Kashmir).

The supply of icon models from the Mahaviharas ceased after the Muslim conquest of the Gangetic plains in 12-13th century A.D. But Himalayan art continued to flourish, more so because many Hindu and Buddhist craftsmen and clergy were obliged to take refuge in Himalayan regions. In absence of newer models, however, the stereotype images tended to become more and more stylized, not only because the artists could do no better, but also because by replicating images according to the canonical precepts they could achieve definite merit. This is the reason why Taranatha, the famous Tibetan historian, could distinguish the various Indian schools in the Himalaya as late as the 16th century. In his *History of Buddhism,* Taranatha identified the Madhyadesha school, the Eastern school, the old Western school and the Kashmiri school. "In Nepal", he states, "the earliest school of art resembled the Old Western school; but in the course of time, a peculiar Nepalese school was formed which in painting and bronze casting resembled rather the Eastern style...... In Kashmir too there were in former times followers of the Old Western school of Madhyadesha; later on, a certain Hsuraja founded a new school of painting and sculpture called the Kashmiri school".

Vajrayana Buddhism finally reached the eastern Himalaya after a long and circuitous journey through central Asia, Nepal and Tibet. It entered Sikkim and Bhutan through Kham, the estern province of Tibet, which was already famous for making beautiful bronzes.

Called the Kham-so (made in Kham), both Sikkim and Bhutan benefited from this technique of bronze casting. The local craftsmen also mastered the central Asian art of making the gigantic statues of clay called *Dzaku*: the practice of making huge figures in clay is said to have originated in the oasis of Khotan where there were no stone quarries. The local genius is moreover apparent in their mastery of details as seen in paintings, specially in the drawings of intricate embroideries and other ornate floral motifs. Above all the native craftsmen excelled in the kind of art which is depicted in *Goinkhangs* or secret rooms reserved for the inmates of the demoniac world.

Particularly in Bhutan, where the Duk-pa sect of Vajrayana was transplanted onto the magic and rituals of the original Bon cult as late as the 17th century A.D., the iconometry of Tantricism was made even more complicated by the introduction of its Shamanistic norms: mountain passes were presided over by a Mountain Spirit; Soil Masters ruled the earth; *Klu* was the spirit of the water springs; *Lha* was the sacred mountain from which the ancestral gods of the family descended. Symbols of such fantastic spirits are often placed on mountain tops and near water springs, making unforgettable impressions in the bizarre surroundings of the Himalaya.

In the execution of the Buddha images however, the artists of both Sikkim and Bhutan continued to follow the ancient precepts as laid down in early Indian treatises. Despite the multiple influences to which the Buddhist art was subjected on its long journey to the eastern

Top : panel depicting the life of the Buddha from Alchi Monastery.
Top right : painting depicting Yama from Lachung Monastery, Sikkim.

Himalaya, it is surprising that the Buddha images did not lose that marvellous simplicity of clear cut and rhythmic surfaces, harmonious proportions and serene facial expressions for which the classical sculptures of the Gupta period are so famous.

Meanwhile in the western Himalaya, new reform movements among the followers of both Hinduism and Buddhism had taken hold of the people's imagination. As against the devotees of Padmasambhava who wore red hats, the new sect of "yellow hats" was led by reformers such as Tsong-kha-pa in the 14th century, who called for greater monastic discipline and a return to the original teaching of the Buddha. In terms of art, the movement focused the artists' attention on basic art forms rather than the complicated Tantric symbols by which they had been overwhelmed. This resulted in the production of some exquisite paintings depicting the life story of the historical Buddha, as well as *Jataka* stories of his reincarnations, as seen in some of the major monasteries in Ladakh.

The visual diversity of Himalayan art, like the mountains themselves, is incredibly wide. The sculptures are carved in all forms of relief, and in painting the variety of colour and design is equally rich. Yet like the hundreds of gods and goddesses of the Hindu and Buddhist pantheons aspiring to the same divine ideals, these magnificent works of art express a remarkable unity in diversity. To find a *leitmotiv* for this fantastic art, one must look beyond its incidental stylistic, mythological, ritualistic and legendary attributes, towards the majestic silvery peaks of primaeval ideals, epitomized by the symbolic pillar of the heavenly vault and the divine yogi of the Himalaya.

Top : Chanak eagle. Above : copper mask from Bhakli.
Opposite page : painting, Pedi Wangmo, Sikkim.

Rabindranath Tagore – a Renaissance man

K. G. SUBRAMANYAM

Opposite page : Rabindranath Tagore in Japan, in 1916. Above : Rabindranath engaged in drawing, a photograph taken in 1937. Above right : one of his paintings—it has an air of fantasy and other worldliness.

The term "Renaissance Man" derives its meaning from what we know of the spirit of the fifteenth century Italian renaissance and the multi-dimensional creativity of some of its central figures. In our times, the term implies a many-sided creative genius who contributes to various fields under the impulse of a total vision. It could also mean a person who radiates a spirit of humanism, giving *man* a pre-eminent place in his value system, investing him with a new sense of freedom and a new sense of responsibility, and raising him from a state of passive resignation to one of self-assured endeavour.

Rabindranath Tagore can be said to be both. He was a creative genius who made contributions to many fields—literature, art, music, drama, education, social reorganisation—and inspired fresh thinking about basic life-values. He was also, in his time, a tireless standard-bearer of human freedom who relentlessly scrutinised prevailing notions regarding man's relationship to man, or to environ-

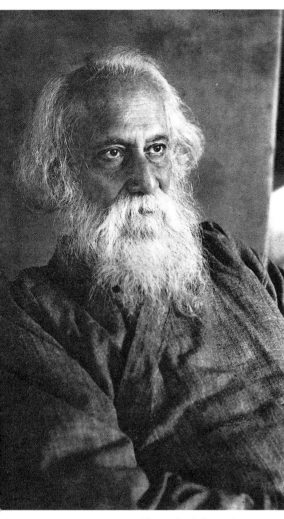

*Above : in Calcutta in 1938.
Right and far right :
Rabindranath Tagore's paintings
and drawings had a powerful
visual impact. His faces and
portraits are masked in mystery;
they are intriguing enigmas, as
seen here.*

ment, or to what is referred to as Supreme Reality. He can also be called a "renaissance man" in a more particular sense—as a man who rode the crest of what is now known as the "Bengal renaissance".

The term "Bengal renaissance" signifies the changes in the attitudes of Indian intelligentsia under western impact, and the activities and institutions that grew out of this. Since Bengal was the main arena of this impact in its first stage, Calcutta being the first administrative stronghold of the British, the initial intellectual ferment was also located there. In the early stages the response of the Indian elite was extreme, in the nature of either total acceptance or stolid resistance. But they soon realised that this came out of their weakness or lack of wisdom. They came to see that the British subjugation of India was as much the result of weaknesses inherent in the Indian society of that time as it was of British cupidity, or of the relative dynamism of British ideas and institutions. They knew that India had an ancient culture with continuous traditions in art, literature and thought, a culture that had been the source of inspiration to the world at large; and so the weakening of Indian society was the result of the weakening or stagnation or mischannelling of these source streams. Therefore, any mature outlook should seek the removal of these weaknesses, the reanimation of healthy source streams and the acceptance of whatever was useful and beneficial from the new impact of the west. Raja Rammohun Roy (1772-1828) can be taken to exemplify this outlook. He tried to study and re-expound the basics of Indian religions. He campaigned against existing social evils and superstitious practices. He pleaded for a modern kind of education that did not over-look or underplay the country's cultural heritage. Rabindranath's grand-father, Dwarakanath Tagore, was a close associate of Rammohun Roy and supported many of his enterprises. His father, Devendranath Tagore, headed, under his inspiration, a reformist Hindu sect which eschewed idol worship and harked back to the monistic vision of the ancient texts of the Upanishads.

By the time Rabindranath (1861-1941) was born, many things had happened on the Indian scene. The British government had taken over the administration of the country from the East India Company. Universities based on the British model had been established in three major cities—Calcutta, Bombay and Madras; and a new educational system had been introduced. Certain social reforms had been enacted by legislation under pressure from the local intelligentsia. Some non-official institutions had sprung up to study and make a critical appraisal of Indian culture in its many facets. Such institutions helped to build an intellectual counter-force that looked askance at many British actions and wanted to liberate the country from their domination. With the spread of education, more and more people found it impossible to tolerate discrimination and injustice; they wanted to assert their democratic rights and express their national identity.

Rabindranath Tagore came on the scene at this point and was destined to play a major role in it. He was born into a very illustrious family. As already stated his grand-father and father were both remarkable men, one a resourceful and progressive entrepreneur, the other a religious reformer. Among his brothers there was a philosopher-poet, a playwright-composer-draughtsman, an administrator—the first Indian member of the Indian Civil Service; one of his sisters was a writer and the editor of a home journal. Two of his nephews were artists and motivators of a new art movement, and one of them was, besides, a writer of a great originality and excellence. So it

was a highly creative family humming with activity, which was aware of what was happening in the world and debated the foremost issues of the day, particularly those related to India's resurgence and its relationship to the rest of the world.

Here, Rabindranath's special stature was marked out from the beginning. Rebelling against any kind of structured tutelage from his very early years, he was independent and sensitive; he took in everything, read voraciously and came to have a distinct personality at a very young age. His first foray into poetry was at the age of eight; his romantic mind responded to a translation of Bernardin de Saint Pierre's "Paul et Virginie" that was being serialized in a journal of that time. At the age of thirteen he translated Shakespeare's "Macbeth" in verse. From the age of fourteen his poems started getting printed under his own name and at the age of fifteen, he wrote his first piece of literary criticism. At sixteen he wrote a series of poems in the manner of the medieval religious lyrics of India; this was a stylistic *tour de force*. From then on he was a noticed poet and literary figure in Bengal. At twenty he came to have a near-mystical vision of the world which glows through all his later work; he recorded this experience in a long poem titled "Awakening of the Fountain". The fountain, once awakened, did not rest. Year after year it poured forth poems, plays, fiction, essays, songs that were sung throughout Bengal, plays that mixed poetry, music and dance with dialogue, and set new trends in the theatre. Presently his collected literary work runs into thirty bulky volumes and his published letters into eleven.

Though the world at large came to know Rabindranath only after he was awarded the Nobel Prize for literature in 1913, he was by then a well-known literary figure in Bengal. He had nearly renovated the Bengali language and brought to it a new range and dimension, embellishing it with a new kind of imagery. Even if the orthodox took

Birth of the river Kaveri at Thalai Kaveri in Karnataka.

The great rivers of India

MANOHAR MALGONKAR

The Rivers of olden days

Open a map of India. The pattern of rivers is like the lines on the palm of a hand. There are, literally, hundreds of rivers. But most of them at some point merge into broader lines to form major river systems. As in any other country, all our rivers, large or small, are like close kinsmen to the people who depend on their waters. But here in India they are something more too—veritable gifts from Mother India herself. Like her they, too, are all women, and again like her they, too, bear a touch of divinity.

All this stems from the fact that India is an ancient land, and that one of our religions, Hinduism, is a very, very old faith. The religion was there, almost in its present form, even before history began to be recorded, and the rivers have always been an inseparable part of it. The collection of hymns called the *Rigveda* which form the very core of that religion, were compiled nearly five thousand years ago. It is so ancient that, according to the Oxford History of India, "it stands quite by itself, high up on an isolated peak of antiquity", something unique, for the simple reason that there is nothing remotely approaching it in sheer bulk, let alone in power or vitality or artistic imagery, to serve as a standard of comparison.

And in the *Rigveda,* there is a section devoted to our rivers. It is called *Nadi-stuti,* which means 'In Praise of the Rivers' and the fact that it mentions only nineteen rivers which belong to the Punjab and the territories immediately to its north and south shows that the Aryan civilization it represents had not penetrated very deep into the Indian subcontinent. One thing we discern from the hymns of *Nadi-stuti* is that our rivers have always been given female names, and that, while virtually all of them have been deserving of their praises being sung, only one or two were held to be sacred.

These early Aryans seemed to know almost as much as we do today about the rivers that traversed their lands. For instance, four of the five rivers which have given the Punjab its name of the 'Land of the Five Rivers' figure in it. They are the Sutudri, the Parushini, the Asikni and the Vitasta, names which have been transformed over the centuries into the Sutlej, the Ravi, the Chenab, and the Jhelum.

Above : the river Yamuna at Agra mirrors the silhouette of the eternal Taj Mahal. Right : the Alaknanda river in the Garhwal Himalayas. Far right : morning mist rises from the upper reaches of the Ganga.

The Indus

Of the nineteen rivers of the *Nadi-stuti* by far the most important is the Sindhu, or the Indus. The hymns trace its source in the high Himalayas near Mount Kailash, and follow it westwards through the forbidding mountain terrain north of Kashmir. They describe how the Indus breaks through the Hindu Kush range to turn southwards towards its meeting with the Arabian Sea still hundreds of kilometres away. They enumerate as many as ten of the Indus's tributaries but say nothing about the immense length of the river which, as we know today, is 2900 kilometres, nor do they explain the vital fact that it is this river, the Indus, which has given our nation its name: India.

But the *rishis* or holy men as also the *pandits* or scholars who composed the hymns of the *Rigveda* cannot be faulted for not pandering to the tyranny of facts and figures. They were men of imagination, even romantics, given to flights of fancy and creating word-pictures rather than recording weights and measures. And we must be thankful to them for telling us many things about the Indus which would have otherwise escaped our notice. That the Sindhu is "a gigantic mass of moving water without a single obstruction in its course through the plains," must have been noticed by less inspired observers too, but would they have also noted the fact that she was "a forever young and beautiful girl dressed in shining garments and decked in gold ornaments," who, from time to time, "roars like a bull"? Or again that this maiden is richly dowered by the Gods with "limitless stretches of land capable of producing vast quantities of nourishing corn and fat sheep with soft wool and a breed of the swiftest horses", and who, because of her munificence, "constitutes a blessing to those who have the good fortune to reside in the land through which she flows."

The Saraswati

All this and more, and rightly so. But that does not mean that the Sindhu was especially holy. More surprisingly, even the Ganga which throughout history has been sacred to the Hindus, had no such connotations in Vedic times. The holiest river of *Nadi-stuti* is Saraswati. It was also the most important and the most powerful—so powerful that its waves could shatter the most formidable obstacles that stood in its way. The Saraswati is showered with praise, one might even say, flattery, and addressed as *Priyatame*, or beloved, *Naditame,* the River of Rivers, and even *Ambitame* which means 'Most reverend of Mothers'.

But where is the Saraswati? No one knows; even *Nadi-stuti* does not tell us where it is, or just takes it for granted that everyone should know. We have to fall back on a legend which says that the Saraswati is the river that joins both the Ganga and Yamuna rivers near Allahabad in northern India to form what is called Triveni-Sangam or confluence of three rivers. However, overground there is no such river. A convenient, if not convincing, answer to the riddle of the Saraswati is that it did exist in Vedic times but has since vanished. If so, it is by no means the only Indian river to have done so. Another well-marked system centering on a river called Hakra or Wahindah on the edge of Western Rajasthan which existed as recently as the eighteenth century has also disappeared. For that matter, most of our major rivers are known to be notoriously temperamental and have changed their courses frequently. "Old beds of the Sutlej can be traced across a space eighty five miles wide," Mr. Vincent Smith, the author of *The Oxford History of India* points out, and the

Above : river sunset at Allahabad. Above right : evening prayers at the Ganga in Haridwar. Right : worshippers offer prayers to the Ganga at Varanasi.

Ganga has strayed all over its extensive stamping ground which is known as the Gangetic plain, and in the process left towns and villages which were once on its banks high and dry and at the same time obliterated others.

The Ganga

But no matter how capricious the Ganga might have shown herself to be, in the Hindu mind it can do no wrong. To a Hindu it is not only the 'River of Life' but also, at the same time, 'The River of Death' for he longs to die beside it, or at the very least to have his ashes after cremation cast in its waters. It is to him what the Saraswati must have been in ancient Vedic times, a sacred body of water.

In describing such a river, statistics can have but little meaning. How many of the million or so pilgrims who flock to the periodic Kumbh melas or holy gatherings at Allahabad would for instance know where the source of the river was or where it joins the sea. That the Ganga rises in an icy Himalayan glen and after flowing nearly 2500 kilometres joins the Bay of Bengal can never be of as much relevance to them as that she represents, as Jawaharlal

Nehru described it, "the very symbol of India's age-long culture and civilization". And that it begins to break up into branches while still 400 kilometres away from the sea, that it passes through some of the most densely populated areas of the world and that it is joined by a dozen or so major rivers is somehow less important than their obsessive conviction that whoever dies in Varanasi, where the Ganga attains supreme holiness, goes straight to heaven.

Nonetheless, some of the facts about the quality of the Ganga's water cannot be lightly dismissed. Scientists have—or say they have—established how its water will keep for a year in bottles and that cholera germs die in it within a few hours, or even that a tank reputed to be fed from the Ganga "has the power of dissolving human bones within three days."

Yet another curious anomaly about the river is that it has gone into maps and gazetteers and geography texts as the river Ganges. As it happens, the *Namavali* or the chain-of-names with which devotees are supposed to invoke the Ganga has as many as 108 appellations, ranging from "Thou who are born from the lotus feet of the

Above : Crowds along the river bank at Haridwar.
Above right : cattle returning home at sunset ford the
Chambal river in central India. Far right : the Marble
Rocks, Narmada river.

God Vishnu," to "Thou who leapest over mountains in sport," but no such names as the 'Ganges'. 'Ganges' was a particularly careless or capricious linguistic distortion on the part of India's British rulers and which must today be regarded as the hundred-and-ninth name of the Ganga.

The Yamuna

To millions of Indians who inhabit the rich, evergreen triangle of land called the Doab, or the country between the Ganga and the Yamuna, the two rivers are sisters, all but inseparable. Indeed, often enough they are spoken of as one, as the Ganga–Yamuna.

Except for a lapse on the part of the British which they took a hundred years to set right, the Yamuna has always been the river of India's capitals. So it was in ancient times when the Pandavas had their capital beside it, and so it is today. The Yamuna sweeps past New Delhi in a majestic arc overlooked by the fort of the Mughals and the tombs and towers of other dynasties. Perhaps it is for this reason that the Yamuna has also witnessed some of the bloodiest and most decisive battles that were fought between great

armies for the possession of supreme power in India. Indeed, one of the towns on its banks, Panipat, which is barely a three-hour bus ride from New Delhi, has been the scene of no less than three major and historic battles that saw such carnage that many people still tend to react to the very sound of the word 'Panipat' with awe.

From the nation's capital, the Yamuna flows on to Mathura, the scene of the boyhood pranks of one of Hinduism's most popular Gods, Krishna, and then on to Agra to serve as a reflecting pool for the Taj Mahal. Between Agra and its confluence with the Ganga, it is joined by virtually all the rivers that flow through the state of Madhya Pradesh, the Chambal, the Sind, the Betwa, the Dahsan and the Ken. But even when glutted with their waters at its meeting place with the Ganga, which is known as the Sangam, the Yamuna still remains very much the younger sister—the Ganga just swallows it up.

The Brahmaputra

It is not until a thousand kilometres further down its course that the Ganga may be said to have met its match,

not in holiness, but in sheer volume of water. That is when it joins the Brahmaputra in the plains of Bangla Desh where both rivers lose their identities and flow on as the mighty Meghna, which surely must be one of the biggest rivers on earth and whose special world of sand and palms and serenity and sudden squalls and tragedy has been so vividly portrayed by Rabindranath Tagore in his novels.

Like the Indus, the Brahmaputra too has its source in the regions of the Kailash Mountain, and, give or take a hundred kilometres, is also of the same length. But here comparisons end. Both flow in opposite directions and reach different seas. The Brahmaputra flows in an eastward direction through the desolate immensities of Tibet and for the first sixteen hundred kilometres of its course even bears a different name, the Tsang-Po. In earlier times, it was believed to have gone underground after reaching the north-east corner of India—at least no one knew what had happened to it. True, a large river emerged out of these same mountains more than a hundred kilometres to the south which was called the Brahmaputra. But that both rivers were one and the same was a matter of debate and conjecture till well past the middle of the last century. How the riddle was finally solved is one of the more romantic adventures of inland exploration.

The search was entrusted to a group of volunteers known as The Pandit Explorers. They were learned men who were sent into Tibet in the guise of pilgrims carrying hidden compasses and barometers. They would record compass bearings and altitudes of the mountains and rivers they passed. So difficult was their undertaking that two or three such journeys were said to constitute a life's work.

One of these intrepid men, Pandit Kintup, was sent to Tibet to trace the course of the Brahmaputra. He was instructed to venture as far as he could go, and there throw into the Tsang-Po pieces of wood cut to a certain shape and size. A close watch was kept for these blocks of wood on the Indian side. Soon after Kintup entered Tibet, however, he was made a prisoner by the Tibetan guards. Two years later, he managed to escape, and such was his

energy and devotion to duty, drove himself on to complete his task. But by now he had been given up for dead, and the watch on the river called off. It was only after his return, nearly four years after his departure, that he was able to convince the authorities that the Brahmaputra and the Tsang-Po were the same.

The Marudvihara and the Kali

Many Hindus believe that the Vedas were actually revealed to us by the gods, complete as they stand. But there can be no doubt that at least that part dealing with the rivers is the work of man. The giveaway is a little quirk of less than divine favouritism on the part of whoever compiled the list: the prominence given to a small stream called Marudvihara which is a tributary of the Chenab high up in an inaccessible Kashmir valley. Clearly, whoever gave it a place among the rivers to be praised must have lived on its banks. In a similar vein, I would myself be tempted to mention a river called Kali in my salutation to our rivers. It flows past my village and has been the scene of some of the most pleasurable moments of my life. It is a very small river, a mere hairline in maps, and not quite a hundred kilometres in length. But it is a playful, dancing river which winds through some of the greenest of India's rain forests, and then plunges down to the sea near Karwar. Herds of wild elephants still sport in its pools, and crocodiles float on its glass smooth surface, looking like logs of wood. I would have no hesitation in addressing the Kali as *Priyatame*, beloved, and, in a moment of ecstasy such as comes from pulling out from its depths a good fish, even *Naditame*, the Ultimate River.

A Peninsula of Rivers

The mention of the Kali in this stream of waters has served as an excuse for a change of scene, from the wide shoulders of the subcontinent to its peninsular portion which is known as the Deccan. In the process we have crossed yet another river, the Narmada, which is regarded as the dividing line between the north and the south.

The Deccan has its own rivers: notably, the Tapi, the Godavari, the Krishna and the Kaveri. Each one of them

is a formidable entity and each has strong claims to deification. A guided tour along all of them is manifestly impossible; a short article does not have enough space even for vital statistics, let alone for an assessment of their contribution through the ages to the life of the land and their place in the emotions of the people. And then again, what of the claims of other rivers? Of the Tungabhadra which once spawned an empire and a culture; the Sheravathi which, in throwing herself down a sheer cliff, has given us the Jog Falls, reputed to be the highest in the world; or again, the Teesta or the Mahanadi or the Sarayu or the Pilar and dozens—scores—of others? Small or large, each has a forceful personality, and formidable claims for special treatment. Some pass through hauntingly desolate ruins, or embrace famous temples or forts, others have thrown up schools of music or of dancing, or generated religious revivals; yet others are the scenes of battles, or serve as sanctuaries for birds, or tigers, or elephants. And each has its devotees, or at least passionate protagonists. The appropriate thing to do is to sign off with a chanting of a Sanskrit verse that a Hindu recites at the time of taking his bath:

गंगेच यमुनेचैव गोदावरी सरस्वती
नमदे सिंधु कावेरी, जले अस्मिन् संनिधम् कुरु

O Ganga, O Yamuna, and also Godavari and Saraswati and Narmada and Sindhu and Kaveri, by your waters I purify myself.

This hymn to the rivers is also a hymn to the nation. Between them these seven (or, if you take away the Saraswati, six) rivers sketch out an image of the land. They highlight its vastness and interpret its imperishable unity. From the burning sands of the Sind desert where the Sindhu flows to the waterlogged swamps called the Sundarbans where the Ganga joins the sea; from the snowbound Himalayan peaks in the north to the end of the peninsula washed by the Kaveri. An invocation to the seven rivers is also a daily act of remembrance and salutation to the land that is traversed and nourished by them: the Motherland herself.

Left : at the confluence of the Ganga and Yamuna at Allahabad. Above : river in the Himalayas. Right : devotee offering fruits to the river.

129

Intimate glimpses of Indian feasts

SHALINI HOLKAR

A large raw fish moves through the streets of Calcutta, dressed and bejewelled for a wedding...

In the marble courtyard of a Rajasthan palace, diamond and pearl-clad courtiers sit down to a snow white banquet...

Cannons boom, videos grind and a number of pigs are prepared for roasting as a tiny island off the coast of Goa prepares for the feast of its namesake...

These events are but a minute sampling of the endlessly varied and interesting approaches to festive celebration in India. Almost every occasion involves food of some sort: be it a feast or a symbolic nibble. A complete discourse on Indian festival foods would consume many volumes. In a limited space, we can only examine little vignettes of feasting, chosen as examples of the sweetness, the excesses, the simplicity, the variety that are all a part of feasting in this country.

The diversities are those of caste, community, climate, custom, geographic location, economic status and personal inclination. Within this diversity, there are a very few celebrations common to the whole of the country. Weddings are the one exception. In some way or the other, weddings are celebrated everywhere in India, though that celebration takes many forms.

When one speaks of sweet things, very close to the heart, it is best to let those who love them use their own words, so we shall now listen as an earnest, middle class Bengali Brahmin family explains why a raw fish moves through the streets of Calcutta on its way to a wedding...

"Fish in Bengal is considered very auspicious, second

Riches from a Bengali table : traditional sweets, above, include rasgullas, sandesh *and* mishti doi. *Above right : auspicious fish decorated for a Bengali wedding.*

Above : Bengali wedding dinner includes fried eggplant, fish and meat curry and fresh tomato chutney. Right : food from a Kashmiri wazwan : gustabas, *meat - balls in a curd sauce and* tabbak maz.

only to rice as an absolute essential in the Bengali diet. So when a young couple is to be married, the bride's family will send a fish to the groom's family on the morning of the wedding. Our custom demands that it should be the finest fish we can afford and that, in order to make it as auspicious as possible, we should dress it like the groom in a fine, cotton *dhoti* with flower garlands round its gills, jewels in its nose, and even sometimes a cigarette in its mouth!

"This is all in fun, of course; everyone laughs and comments as it goes through the streets to the house of the groom. His family will keep it and prepare it for one of the feasts, so the bride's side also sends cooking utensils and the oil in which to prepare it. But there is another meaning to the gift. Along with the fish comes a small box of turmeric powder. The groom's family will take a bit of this auspicious powder, touch it to the feet of their son and return it to the bride's house straightway; for both must now rub themselves in turmeric powder and bathe in preparation for the wedding.

"The actual wedding takes place in the morning; that night comes the feasting, the part everyone loves. There will be folding chairs and long, wooden tables, covered in absorbent paper. The food is eaten from *sal pattas*, plates made of leaves stuck together with twigs. Water is served in earthenware tumblers.

"The young men of the bride's family tie clean towels around their waists and serve the food. We could go on forever about the food; but to be very brief, the banquet starts with fried foods: perhaps potatoes or eggplant, then comes the *luchi* or little fried breads, then fried fish and a thick, chick pea soup. Next there is a mixed vegetable called *labra*, a rice pullao, and then fish curry in a rich gravy.

"This is only the beginning. There follows a special mutton dish, after which everyone refreshes his palate with a fresh chutney of tomato, onion, and dried fruits and nuts, flavoured with a healthy dose of mustard seed and red chilli powder. Wafer thin fried *papads* mark the end of the savories and the beginning of the sweets, the course dearest to every Bengali's heart.

"If we can afford it, we will offer five sweets at a wedding dinner; but even the humblest feast will have at least *ras gullas*, if not the *sandesh*, *kala jamun*, *chanas* and *mishti doi*. Sometimes the sweet course alone takes up as much time as the rest of the meal put together!"

One leaves this Bengali family reluctantly. The spirit of wedding feasts is the same all over India: the joy, the togetherness, the pride and the participation; but there the similarity ends, as it does with all Indian feasts. Nothing, for example, could be less like a Bengali Hindu wedding feast than a wedding feast in a Muslim family of Kashmir.

Kashmir has one particular style of feast called *wazwan*, which appears at weddings, as well as other auspicious occasions, particularly religious occasions. The origins of *wazwan* are lost in the crisscross of history, somewhere between Russia, Persia, and Kazakhstan; but the *wazwan* dishes are now unique unto themselves; the *akhni*, *rogan josh*, and *tabbak maz*; and the Kashmiri spinach, lotus root and crisp turnips which accompany this solid cuisine. Whereas the feasts of hot, humid Bengal are based on fish and light vegetables, those of this high, Himalayan land are firmly meat-based, with sauces rich in the produce of the region: almonds and walnuts; wondrous milk; thick curd, sweet, hot chillis and the famous saffron of the Kashmiri foothills.

Vegetables play a very minor role in *wazwan*; sheep is

the star of the show. Preparation for an evening *wazwan* begins in the early morning. The *wazas*, or cooks, arrive with all their utensils and the heavy, copper pots which belong to their association. The host supplies them with all the spices and condiments they require; also with kilos of clarified butter for cooking. They set up their fires in long trenches in the compound and the butcher goes to work with his assistants, cutting the sheep so expertly that every part may be used, producing as many as thirty or forty different meat dishes in one *wazwan*.

The compound is alive with activity. Someone stokes the fires, someone stirs, someone takes a break to pull on the everpresent 'hooka'. Two men do nothing but pound fat into the ground meat which will become the *gustabas* the crowning glory of the meal, and the dish which signals the end of the *wazwan*. *Gustaba* are round meat balls, the size of a small orange, flavoured with the seeds of black cardamom and simmered in a sauce of rich curd, sheep broth and the five heating spices: clove, cardamom, cinnamon, bay leaf and anise.

Guests, who have been seated in fours around *thrambis* or large eating trays, gather up the last bits of rice with their fingers, mixing it with the succulent gravies, and reflect with satisfaction on the *marzwangan* and *dhaniwal kormas*, the long, Kashmiri *kabobs*, the excellent green walnut and fresh mint chutney, as well as the dozens of other dishes which the *wazas* have ladled from their big, copper cauldrons into the beaten silver *thrambis*.

It is not unusual to have a thousand guests at a *wazwan*. Many of the older Kashmiri homes have large halls especially for this purpose. Everyone sits on the floor. Women and men will take their meals separately; but both will be clothed in the big, embroidered woollen *pherins*, the heavy jewellery and wonderfully worked shawls for which Kashmir is famous. After the *wazwan*, *cawa*, or Kashmiri tea, is poured into thin, china bowls or tiny glasses from a large, silver samovar. Fresh almonds, a bit of cinnamon, perhaps some threads of saffron perfume the *cawa* and linger on the breath as guests relax.

We shall leave them there in the Himalayas and shift to an island off the coast of Goa, far to the south of Bombay.

It is a Christian feast day on the island, the biggest feast of the year, in honour of the island's patron saint and namesake, St. Jacinto. Our host is a native of that tiny Catholic island. He belongs to one of the seven fishing families who still run trawlers off the coast for a living.

"The feast is celebrated on the second Sunday of May. There are lots drawn amongst all of us who are over fifty in age. If my name is drawn, I am the host and I must pay for the whole thing, the church expenditure, the feast, the band, the video, everything! I must spend as much as I can afford. And I must invite the whole island, two or three hundred people, including those who have gone away to live and only come back once a year for this feast.

"We must make the arrangements one month, two months before: The rice, the spices, (chili, black pepper, clove, cumin, saffron powder), the garlic, the ginger, the oil: we must order all those things and keep them in our house long before the day of the feast. The rice will never be the thick type we use everyday. For feast days we use much lighter, longer rice. From this, we make *arroz*, that is, rice with hot, red Goan pork sausage.

"The people who come to cook this food are all professionals; one lady will make the *sorpatel*, one the beef, one the mutton. And there will be a man, the number one cook, to supervise. Usually he is a retired *taroti*: a Goan who has worked on ships outside Goa all his life and come back here to retire. He knows quite well how to cook for many people; also he likes to keep busy and earn a little money. So he is in charge of the feast, and we must give him everything, especially his food and his drink while he cooks.

"The cooks will come two days before to the island. They will see to everything; organize the compound and the cooking vessels. Many of us have our old family copper vessels, but some now use heavy aluminium. Sometimes the cooks will bring certain things with them; but generally the animals, the pigs, mutton, and all that, we use from our own livestock in the compound. The menu? Well, there will always be some gravy mutton, like *xacuti*, then roast beef, whole pig stuffed with bread and all the ingredients, English style; then salad and maybe fish mayonnaise. But in Goa, there must always be the two favourite pork dishes: *vindaloo* and *sorpatel*. Without them the feast cannot start!

"We use a special *feni* vinegar for the *vindaloo*; the same *feni*—coconut toddy—we give to the cooks and the band while they are working. But usually we drink Goan beer, which we love because of the water. You see, the water in Goa is the most important thing. That makes all the difference to the taste of the food. On our island, we have a wonderful well, spring water, which all of us use only for drinking and cooking. That well is blessed by St. Jacinto. And we maintain it by auctioning the coconuts and caju nuts in the church compound and by the rent we get from allowing outside trawlers to moor near our island.

"You see, until they made the bridge very recently, we were cut off from the mainland; we had to walk across at low tide or go by canoe. It was beautiful, the most beautiful climate. And everyone today still loves to come for our feast. Some stay for the full four days, from Friday evening, when we start to be a little merry, to Saturday vespers, to Sunday when we have the High Mass and then the feast in the afternoon. After that Mass, we fire small cannons that have always been in the church compound. When they hear that 'Boom!' 'Boom!', then everyone on the mainland knows it's our feast, the second Sunday of May.

"After that feast, we very rarely have sweets, usually just fruits: bananas and oranges, but sometimes we make

Opposite page : Kashmiri wazwan *with meat curry and long kebobs : in the background is the spiced tea,* cawa. *Above :* doodh ka sharbat *and* wooli *rice cooked with lentils and meat, both from Hyderabad.*

sannas. Sannas are steamed sweets made of rice ground in toddy with coconut juice. We make those for Christmas too; but St. Jacinto is the big day on our island. We dance till five o'clock in the morning!''

On the opposite coast of India, in Tamil Nadu, a serene saree clad woman with flowers in her hair tells us of her community's special feast day. She speaks with as much love and pride as our Goan friend, yet her community's feast resembles his only in spirit. It is different in every other way. She is a member of the Hindu Nagarathar Chettiar community. Traditionally a cattle raising community, the Nagarathars are now very successful in big city business, though they still retain ties with their seventy-two ancestral villages.

"Our community worships Lord Ganesh, the elephant god. We celebrate his festival twenty-one days after the full moon of November, when the kernels of rice in the newly sown rice crop will just be filling with sweetness. The ceremonies we perform on this festival day bring Lord Ganesh's blessings upon our crop and our household and upon the coming year.

"Lord Ganesh is very fond of a particular pancake called *Karupatty Panniharam*, which we must make for him on this day. But before we prepare these little pancakes, we must observe a special fast for several days, then clean the kitchen thoroughly, remake the earthern cooking hearth

Rituals and ritual food : modak from Maharashtra during the Ganesh Chaturthi festival.

The circle and the triangle

PUPUL JAYAKAR

Tantra and alchemy have co-existed in India from an archaic past and have provided a foundation and a vital resource for craft insight and technology. The Tantric seers or Siddhas, seeking to comprehend natural laws and material phenomena and to evolve physical and psychical instruments to probe and penetrate into the secrets of life and energy, evolved aural and visual symbols in which to contain the imponderables. Finding them in the mystery and magic of austere abstractions, in *mantra* and *yantra*, they saw that the absoluteness of the geometric form gave it a symmetry that could never be fractured. Identical from all sides, nothing could be added to it, nothing taken away.

The most ancient worship of the primeval source of energy, the ancient yet ever young earth mother, was through hieroglyph. Ancient texts which codify magical formulae describe the virgin mother assuming different forms—in times of creation the form of a triangle, in times of preservation the form of a straight line, similarly in destruction she was manifest as the circle.

The triangle, a geometric form which uses a minimum of lines to enclose space and create form, symbolises the earth in its very aspect of sprouting or "coming to be". As the holder of energy, the triangle is the *yoni*, the tool of creation. "The triangular Shakti pervades all beings and brings forth species." In this form she appears as a triangle pointing downwards with a red dot at the centre.

The circle was an outer visualization of cosmic energy. It became the supreme symbol of two pervading energy forms, the virgin goddess and the rising young Sun in the East. The goddess was Chakra Rupa, in the form of a circle; and the word *mandala* itself is another word for the Sun as the exploding life-giving force.

The circle, when reduced to its ultimate point, was the

Above : a dramatic moment in the casting of the charakku — the pouring of the molten metal into the mould.
Top right : model of the charakku or cauldron.

Top right : Kandan Moosari and his wife turn the clay mould, which is in the shape of a vertical wheel.
Top : applying bee-wax to the clay.
Above : the handles of the cauldron, which were separately moulded, are fixed to the body of the clay.

Bindu or dot. Both male and female, the Bindu was the creative unmanifest. The white dot was lunar and male. The red dot was fiery and female. The merging of the two was the cause of the world. The explosion of the red fiery Bindu released the *Nada*, the reverberating sound that filled the universe. This *Nada* or subtle sound was unmanifest and inarticulate. Its movement was upwards, and its reverberations brought forth *Shristi Bija*—the seed of creation, and *Samhar Bija* or the seed of destruction. From *Shristi Bija* arose the five elements: sky, air, water, fire and earth. Nature and its manifestations, including what was made by the hand of man, were *Sakala*, held in time, and therefore inherent in it was *Samhar Bija*, the seed of destruction.

As in most ancient civilizations, craft technology in India was an act of creation, involving doing, knowing and being. The craftsman as the creator of the gods, a con-

ceiver of form and attribute, had an honoured and unique position. The Shilpa texts that codify archaic perceptions were considered divine revelations. The word *Shilpakar* in itself denoted the creator craftsman and included dancers, musicians, makers of icons, acrobats, jugglers, metalsmiths and potters etcetera.

An immensely old school of philosophy, the Sankhya, based on the conservation, transformation and dissipation of energy, as also concepts of space and time, described the ultimate ground of the universe and all manifestation as Prakriti, the first cause, the female principle, primeval matter, holding within it both the expressed and the pre-expressed, without beginning and without end. Within her lay dormant, the potential seed of sprouting. The root meaning of the word "Pra-Kriti" was Pra or excellent, Kriti or creation, excellent creation.

The three constituents of Prakriti were in a state of total equilibrium. They were Satva, essence or luminous intelligence, with the tendency to manifestation, for reflection, but without mass or gravity and therefore unable to manifest. Tamas, matter, mass, gravity, volume and density, containing the ingredients of manifestation, but with inertia which made any independent movement or action impossible. And Rajas, energy, the moving principle, that could counteract and disperse the inertia of Tamas. When touched by Rajas as energy, the inertia inherent in Tamas as matter, mass and gravity was overcome. The process of evolution and the coming into being of the universe was by challenge to Prakriti as equilibrium—by the touch of Purusha, as the luminous, the male immutable principle. What triggered the happening is never satisfactorily explained.

Every phenomenon was a transformation of energy caused by the disturbance in the equilibrium of these

Top : the cauldron is turned upside down with openings for the wax to flow out and the metal to flow in. The mould is enclosed in tiles.

Above : before the commencement of the most crucial stage, rituals to propitiate Bhagvati Kali, the essence of fire as energy, are undertaken.

Top right : the central pit, encircled by fire before the casting of the charakku.

three elements of Satva, Rajas and Tamas. A play of these three coming together and moving apart was the bringing of form out of non-being, out of its pre-manifest state, to a state of revealing or manifestation. The infinite manifestations of the world arose from the multiple ways the three came together—the one playing a dominant role.

These three *gunas* could neither be created nor destroyed. The totality of mass and energy was forever constant.

The founder of the Sankhya school was a mythical being, Kapila, meaning the red one, described as a Siddha or alchemist sage, who first revealed the Sankhya to an Asuri or a woman belonging to the Asura tribe. The Asuras, an iron-smelting tribe, were familiar to the sages of the Rig Veda. They were regarded with an attitude of fearful attraction and dread by the Aryan settlers who recognised in them mighty shamans, masters of fire, with intimate knowledge of metals and a capacity to transform the seemingly immutable. Regarded as healers, capable of both giving and destroying life by their knowledge of herbal secrets, they had gained mastery of transformation and metamorphosis and could change themselves into streams, birds and animals.

Pushed back from their northern domain by the conquering nomadic Aryan tribes, the Asuras finally found refuge in Chhota Nagpur, where they continue to this day their ancient craft of iron smelting, using archaic processes for forging metals. Minerals and metals share in the sacredness attached to the Earth Mother. A crude lump of iron ore is the most archaic symbol of Shakti as dormant primeval energy. Iron, the youngest of the metals, enjoys magico-religious status in India.

A secret, even religious relationship has existed between the craftsman and the ores on which he worked. The magical nature of metals was evident in all primitive tribes. There was an awareness that ores were born in the darkness of the depth of the earth—they had life and ripened in earth's womb.

Amongst the most archaic of the metalsmiths to survive in India were the Kammalars of Tamil Nadu and Kerala. The word "Kammalar" means the maker of an article pleasing to the eye. Five types of craftsmen formed the Kammalar community. They were the Asaris—carpenters, Kalhasaris—masons, blacksmiths, goldsmiths, cobblers and the Moosaris or bellmetal workers. Proud and dignified with ancient faces, holders of creative skill and insight, the Kammalars claimed descent from Vishwa Karma, the divine architect, and at one stage considered themselves equal to Brahmins and insisted on performing and presiding over their own rituals of marriage and birth. It is likely that as aspects of the divine creators, as masters of fire and transmuters of metals, they held a unique position in ancient Dravidian hierarchy.

The Moosaris once gathered in Delhi to undertake the hazardous task of casting a charakku or sacred metal cauldron used in rituals in the temples of Kerala. The vast charakku was seven feet in diameter.

The cauldron goes back to the beginnings of form, when in all ancient civilizations it was regarded as the symbol of the feminine, of birth and the womb.

The chief of the Moosaris was Kandan Moosari, a white-bearded artisan, a silent venerable human being with the sandal marks of a Shiva devotee on his forehead. With him was his wife, Parvathy Kandan. The casting of the charakku by the sanctified Moosaris and their families had been a sacred ritual to be performed within the courtyard of their homes, no outsider being permitted under any circumstances to witness the process. No mechanical instruments for measurement were used by the Moosari.

Nor were there any written instructions on proportions of clay or metal. The size of the wooden axle, the spokes, the quantity of clay, wax, metal was decided by the Moosari out of his vast comprehension and experience, inherited, learnt, observed.

A thatched roof structure in the form of the simplest of the temples of Kerala had been built, under which the charakku was made, the ground being consecrated and made sacred.

The ritual for the casting of the charakku commenced with the Namboodri Brahmins performing the auspicious Ganesh Puja. As this charakku was to be cast in the presence of many people, photographed and filmed, the sanctity of the ritual had to be protected by a special ceremony to the nine constellations, the Navgrahas. From early days of metal casting the Navgrahas had been the guardians of the ritual and closely linked with the six metals and three alloys, gold, silver, iron, lead, tin, bronze, brass and bellmetal. The Namboodri Brahmins piled nine heaps of varied grain, one for each constellation upon nine different coloured cloths. On the Moon, white rice on a black and white checkered cloth. On Mars, Arhar grain, yellow in colour, on a pink cloth. On Mercury, Moong grain on a green cloth. On Jupiter, horse gram, brownish yellow in colour, on a yellow cloth. On Venus, Rajma, a reddish brown *dal* on a white cloth. On Saturn, sesame seed on a blue cloth. On the Sun, golden coloured wheat on a red cloth. On Rahu, Urad, a blackish green grain on a black cloth, and on Ketu, Masoor, a brown gram on a white cloth with signs on it.

A pit was dug at the side of the thatched roof and a wooden pillar was placed in the pit. As it was a very large charakku, it was lathe-turned. The first clay core mould was made with sticky red clay from the banks of the river, mixed with the husk of raw rice. This was kneaded into a fine paste, the grit and stones being removed. A cone in the form of a cylinder with a hole through it was moulded. The craftsman started giving shape and extending the mould like on a potter's wheel from the base of the cylinder. Every round completed was dried before another round was added. An axle called Achuthadi in the form of a wooden wheel with a rod passing through it was inserted through the hole in the clay cone, and both sides of the rod fitted to two wooden stands. As the clay mould became larger, it was fixed to the lathe by twelve wooden spokes. As the work progressed, the mould took the form of a vertical wheel. The hands of the Moosari touched the turning clay mould with delicacy and reverence, his attention unwavering. The eyes followed the hands, the ears were awake for the slightest sound. The body was tuned to the turning of the wheel. The red clay was followed by a layer of black burnt clay. This clay was from previous moulds that had been fired and had remnants of metal in its body. The clay mould continued to turn, guided by the hands of the Moosari; wire was wound round the mould as it formed, to create fine grooves, as also to hold the clay in place. Each day the clay layer that had been applied was allowed to dry, the red and black clay being applied alternatively. When the clay vessel had finally taken shape, it had the form of a vast cauldron.

The next stage was the applying of bee wax to which had been added aromatic resin and castor oil. These three ingredients were heated, and filtered through fine cotton cloth into a vessel of cold water. The wax formed a thick flat surface on the water. It was removed, kneaded and rolled into discs to the thickness of the metal to be used. The wax was of a dark grey colour.

The waxing was done by the Moosari, by applying the discs on to the clay while turning the mould on the wooden axle. The Moosari rotated the mould towards him with infinite care, touching the heated edge of an iron rod to the wax so that the wax was evenly applied. When the wax was dry, a second layer of pure bee wax, white in colour, was applied so that every blemish became visible and could be corrected. At this stage the handles which had been moulded separately were fixed and on the body of the cauldron were placed images of a lizard, symbol of the goddess of prosperity, a crocodile and the sun and the moon.

A layer of red burnt clay was now applied as an outer coating, sufficiently thin to find its way into every detail of the wax. Several coatings of this fine layer of clay were applied—the final coating being of rice husk mixed with clay on the surface of which pieces of burnt pottery were fixed. A number of openings, directly connected with the wax, were left open—one for the wax to flow out, the others for the molten metal to flow into the mould.

The circular base of the vessel was separately moulded in clay with inlets for the pouring of metal. No wax was used to prepare the space on the base of the cauldron but pieces of square smooth brick were placed on the clay core, the cauldron being turned upside down. Before pouring the metal the clay base was fitted; between the clay base and the mould, a space was left for the metal.

All the inlets or openings were kept covered with clay cones, so that no dust could enter the mould, and were only removed when the molten metal was ready.

The charakku being the largest to be cast in living memory, special care had to be taken by the Moosari to see that no flaw marred the perfection of the casting. The auspicious day was determined by astrologers. The ritual casting took place in darkness at the depth of night. It was only in darkness that the colour of the flame and the crucible could be perceived directly and with clarity. The ritual could not be performed on the night of the new moon nor on the darkest lunar night. Before the commencement of the most crucial stage of the process, rituals to propitiate and evoke Bhagvati Kali as Shakti, the most ancient of the ancients, the essence of fire as energy, were undertaken by Kandan Moosari.

And now in the making of the charakku, the time had come to detach the clay mould from its axle. The cauldron was lifted and placed in a pit, with the outlet for the wax to flow out kept clear. Seven pits radiating from the central core to correspond to the seven rays of the sun were dug. Kandan Moosari descended into the pit facing East and lit the first fire, to the sound of chanting. The mould was then surrounded by clay tiles. When the mould was red hot, the wax started to flow from the outlet that had been left clear.The wax flowed into containers and could be re-used. Again it was the instinct of the Moosari that determined whether the wax was fully drained. A mistake and the casting would be irretrievably flawed. The draining over, the opening through which the wax had flowed out was then closed with burnt clay.

By now forty of his kinsmen from Kerala had gathered. The elders of the tribe entered into earnest discussion. On the night of the casting, the clay mould, which was now free of wax, was heated in a pit till it assumed the redness of glowing charcoal. If too hot, the vessel would crack; if not hot enough, the molten metal would not have an even

flow. Eight hundred kilos of metal scrap were placed in crucibles made of burnt clay and charcoal of rice husk. The crucibles were then placed in twelve earthen ovens; lighted by flames, dark skinned bodies intertwined, moving from furnace to mould, steel rods raked the fires, bellows stoked the flames. Kandan Moosari had used no measurement to determine the amount of molten metal needed to replace the wax in the casting of the charakku nor were there any instruments to measure temperature. As he commenced the final process, every sense was awake and operating. The Moosari and the elders watched like hawks the changing colour of the flames of the molten metal. When the flame burnt blue like a peacock's throat, it was ready.

In a frenzy of activity yet like dancers in perfect coordination, the youngest Moosaris turned to the mould, removing the sherds, opening the conduits. And now live flames, red green in colour, sprang pure through the outlets. The whole area encircled by furnaces appeared aflame.

The chief of the Moosaris paused, his mind like a bird on wing, motionless in flight, seeking no nest nor direction. The Moosari observed the red crucible and the intense blue of the flame. For him colour as the goddess was awake. As master of fire, his undisturbed perception would determine perfection or destruction. In the instant before the blue hot molten metal flowed, the artisan sage was the luminous principle of intelligence. In that instant prior to creation he touched the unmanifest ground from which all manifestation, the "coming to be", is. The million years of past, present and future existed simultaneously. In the very intensity of his perception the atoms of the metal and the earth crucible were changing and taking form.

The Moosari faced East, as he commenced the pouring of the metal. The blue flame entered and united with the red green flame emanating from the glowing earthen crucible. And as the Moosari and the elders poured, half the outlets were left untouched, to ensure that the hot air could flow out. The pouring was continuous, the watchfulness did not cease. The operation took several hours. The crucibles were small and the pouring had to be even and smooth so that the metal ran unseen through the whole cauldron, into every crevice, and into every groove. Nothing was trivial, for the minutest flaw in the pouring would mean that the vessel would shatter.

The pouring ended, the Moosari and the elders stood back. A sense of reverential awe, of mystery, pervaded the craftsman and the ground of the creative. Energies and primeval forces had taken over. For seventyfive days Kandan Moosari had lived in intimate contact with the process of creation. His attention had never wavered. With the pouring, the miracle of birth and form had taken place. His function as the creator had ended. Within the darkness of the red hot earth, the original home of all life, the metal, like an embryo, would cool, solidify, gain density and form. The atoms of the metal would rearrange themselves in the shape of their earthen womb. And when the mould cooled and the cast was broken after prayer and ritual, the sacred cauldron would be revealed. Essence, energy and mass in ultimate union.

The birth of form and the technology needed for its manifestation has always demanded the seer, the scientist as the explorer into physical matter, and the craftsman, the creator of form, to come together in relationship. This alone creates a milieu where insight, transmutations of matter, the tools of technology and skill as excellence in action, coalesce; that instant is the anonymous birth of the

creative, of the presencing of form, of luminous revelation.

Sankhya provided a philosophy based on an observation of nature, of the behaviour of mass and the potency of energy. Sankhya held a hard material view of origins, with a profound interest in the ultimate constituents of matter. This approach to the pre-manifest and the instant of "coming to be" laid the foundations of physical and chemical phenomena from which the artisan drew sustenance and skill.

Tantra had links to the earth, and to agricultural magic and ploughing. Tantra was also linked to alchemy with its minute observation of inner and outer phenomena, as well as its concern with transformation of energy, within the mind and in the crucibles of the laboratory. Tantra gave to the artisan craftsman a vocabulary of space, colour, sound and density—the ingredients of all form.

Skill arose out of the relationship between the craftsman and his tools and his material, and from his capacity for unwavering attention; insight was essence, the flowing of the stream of observation.

Some time ago I had the privilege of discussing the nature of insight and skill with Krishnamurti, one of the most profound minds of our age. During discussion one perceived that the movement of insight was a voyage into time, into the past, limitless. The awakening of insight

Above : bell metal charakku, probably from 17th to 19th century, now at the State Museum, Trichur.

demanded a seeing, listening, which was the awakening of all the senses simultaneously, so that, in that instant, fragmentation ended. The senses flowing simultaneously was a state of flowering, an awakeness, in which the barriers of the within and the without cease to exist. A state which perceives an object, the "what is", with all the senses alive, apprehends objects without that perception being held or transformed by the object. And so the flow of seeing, listening, continues without obstacle to inhibit it or give it direction.

Unlike other instruments of mind which turn to the storehouse of personal knowledge as memory, exploring, discarding, analysing, to find a perception without bondage; insight does not search. It sees the within and the without of object, grasps it as a whole. This seeing is the creative ground that makes luminous and reveals. In this state the holistic is the perception. Out of this arises insight and skill in action. Insight and skill moving together and the environment providing tools and material, visual and aural resources, manifestation and the presencing of the formless is inevitable.

The Gardens of Paradise

SATISH GROVER

"If there is paradise on Earth, it is here, it is here" (Sa'adi)

To the great Mughal Emperor Shah Jahan as he sat on his Peacock Throne in the Red Fort at Delhi and gazed at the scene before him, the palace garden that he built must have seemed like heaven. Emerald trees and fragrant flowers, sparkling rivulets of water coursing down sandstone waterways, graceful marble pavilions looking down on shimmering pools sprayed by lotus fountains, and at night, coloured lamps twinkling behind silvery curtains of cascading water; the Imperial gardens in the Red Fort, as the Persian poet had said, were indeed a paradise on earth. In landscape design, as in other art forms, the Mughal emperors passionately elaborated on Persian tradition to eventually create a brilliant facet of Indo-Islamic art.

The idea of paradise as a garden is one of mankind's oldest myths. It harks back to the oldest traditions of the Near-Eastern dwellers, inspired by reverence for running water and verdant oases amid barren stretches of desert. It appears in the mythology of several religions including Christianity, Judaism, Zoroastrianism and Islam as a vision of an eternal, protected, tranquil space. Persia was the cultural well spring from where a steady stream of arts, letters, courtly style and noble graces found their way to the Mughal court. From Persia was derived the excessive formality of Mughal social and courtly life, austere and orderly, dependent on the belief in the unity of God. Guided by the laws of mathematics and geometry, the rulers of medieval Iran exulted in the formality and symmetry of their paradise gardens, their systematic arrangements of water channels, and their orderly, harmonised layout of flowering and evergreen trees. In India these traditions combined with the intense love of the Mughals for nature in all its variety and profusion. Although the love of trees, flowers and nature was as deep-rooted in Hindu and Buddhist cultures, and Feroz Shah Tughlaq, a fore-runner of the Mughals is credited with having built over a hundred gardens, it was with the grand Mughals that gardens became an obsession, perhaps a spiritual slaking of their nomadic thirst.

This restlessness, this search for peace and security, perhaps forms the *raison d'etre* for the paradise garden in India. Babur, the first of the great Mughals, had lived a rugged life as a fugitive in the hostile environment of the Hindu Kush mountains. Exposed to the dust and heat of the Indian plains, he yearned for the coolness and natural beauty of Ferghana and Samarkand, the home of his younger days. "One of the great defects of Hindustan being its lack of running waters," he said, "it kept coming to my mind that waters should be made to flow by means

The geometrical symmetry of the Mughal garden—Humayun's Tomb in Delhi, the first of the great tomb-gardens.

157

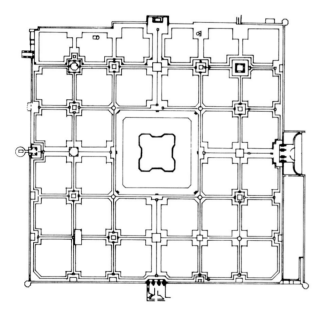

Top : Shalimar Gardens in Kashmir—the unique terraced char-bagh *created by Jahangir. Above right : causeway in Sikandra leads to the strong architecture of Akbar's tomb. Above : plan showing layout of Humayun's tomb.*

of wheels erected wherever I might settle down; also that grounds should be laid in an orderly and symmetrical way." The curious mixture of warrior, poet and victim of capricious natural forces made him look upon nature as something to be conquered and tamed before it could be enjoyed like a poem in peace and tranquillity. His natural affinity with plants and meticulous eye for detail, coupled with an aggressive energy, made him the quintessential gardener, under whose exacting supervision a number of very ordinary and often unfavourable sites were transformed to splendorous landscapes. Ram Bagh on the banks of the river Yamuna in Agra, speculated to be the first garden built by Babur, is the forerunner of a spectacular series of Mughal gardens in India.

The simplest design of the paradise garden is the *charbagh* (literally four gardens, or the four-fold garden) in which water is shown symbolically and organically as the source of life. Four water channels, representing the four

rivers of life, intersect at the central point of the garden. This formed the site of the royal pavilion, and with the development of tomb-gardens, the funerary monument was also located at this focal point. The four quarters representing the four parts of the earth were often divided and sub-divided by minor water courses. Straight lines of trees were planted alongside the stone and marble bordered water channels, which were raised above the garden level to allow underground water to course freely along the garden, irrigating trees and plants. The whole area was enclosed by a wall for privacy and protection from heat and dust. The grass grew in manicured, geometrically defined areas, crisscrossed by the offshoots of the main water channels.

During Jahangir's reign, the junctions of the water channels evolved into shallow fountained pools surrounded by terraces, or *chabutras,* furnished with carved stone benches. Elaborately decorated and covered partitions became important in garden layouts. Perhaps it is this architectural feature that has ensured the survival of most of these historic landmarks, despite the passing of 400 years since their construction.

The formal scheme of the gardens is based on concepts of mathematics and geometry and a philosophical belief in the unity of God and man, which is symbolized by the central point of intersection. Over the decades, the Mughal garden elaborated on the design of its simpler antecedents, and made use of other geometric forms to reflect more complex aspects of Islamic thought. Thus, pavilions were often built in the shape of an octagon, a form evolving from the squaring of the circle where the square represented the material aspect of man, and the circle, eternity. Gardens were also divided into eight parts representing the eight levels towards the attaining of paradise, or the eight divisions of the Qoran. The concept of the garden as symbolic of the cosmic order of the

Above : lake and mountain form the backdrop for the Shalimar Gardens. Opposite page : one of the most spectacular of all Mughal gardens : the perfection and purity of the Taj Mahal, set in a char-bagh.

universe which existed according to divine law was also expressed in other details (even though the monotheism of Islam rejected idealization of nature, and therefore of some of the symbolism attached to gardens). Cypress and fruit trees were alternately grown along the water channels, the evergreen cypress representing immortality, and the flowering fruit trees symbolizing regeneration and a periodic renewal of life. The fusion of mind and matter reached its ultimate expression when the rigid geometric patterns and elements defining garden layouts were consciously overlaid with the informal and natural growth of plants and flowering shrubs. Through their gardens, the Mughals patronised the careful science of horticulture. New varieties of fruits, flowers and trees such as the peach, *chinar*, cherry and apple were propagated, and considerable thought went into the mix and match of planting a garden. There were sun or day gardens, full of the exuberant and glowing colours of *chinar* trees and fruit blossoms, as well as moon or light gardens renowned for the varieties of delicately fragrant shrubs and flowers, such as the jasmine or *chameli, juhi* and *raat ki rani,* (queen of the night).

The design of the *char-bagh* evolved around the efficient use of water and was influenced by the irrigation systems of Persia which defined a wide variety of ways in which water could be used and re-cycled. A high level of ingenuity and engineering skill was displayed in coping with the extremes of water scarcity in the plains, and on the other hand, a vigorous abundance of the same element in the hills.

The varied terrain of Kashmir, with its cascading

waterfalls, numerous perennial springs and spectacular scenery, presented a challenge quite opposite to that which was to be overcome in the dusty north Indian plains, scorched in summer and deluged by rains in the monsoons. Thus, steeply terraced *char-baghs* built by Jahangir in Kashmir are laid around swift-flowing natural streams which serve as the central water course. And again, in deference to the impressive scale of mountain and lake, the enclosing wall, so essential in the dusty plains, was often removed or modified to allow the garden and landscape to merge with one another.

Essentially, the Mughals built three varieties of gardens: the terraced *char-baghs* or paradise gardens; the tomb-gardens, set in square, flat *char-baghs*; and palace gardens, which achieved their height of magnificent elegance in the walled palace garden of Shahjahanabad at the Red Fort in Delhi. The use of large *char-baghs* on a single level as the setting for monumental tombs was the most important innovation in garden architecture introduced by the descendants of Babur. These were usually square in plan, with no terraces but only a slight slope to allow for the water system to follow gravitational forces, as can be seen in the tomb of Humayun. The paradise garden was a parallelogram with a *char-bagh* on each terrace. The early gardens were dependent upon wells with Persian wheels or *rehants;* later, construction of canals drawn from major rivers provided a more dependable water supply, and water courses were then widened to broad shallow channels interspersed with fountains and pools.

It was during the sixteenth and seventeenth centuries under the six great Mughal rulers that the paradise garden blossomed. Curiously this period coincides with the high point of garden making all over the world. In the west, the great Italian Renaissance tradition was reflected in the Villa Lante (1564) and in the Far East, the culture of Japanese garden building was perfected in the Katsura Imperial Villa at Kyoto.

The tradition of formal gardens reached its zenith of exuberance and stylistic perfection under Jahangir and Shah Jahan. Over the decades the changes in structure and decoration, while following the personal inclinations of rulers, were also indicative of the increasing splendour and pageantry of the Mughal empire. Babur's gardens had served him as functional palaces reminiscent of the great outdoor encampments of Central Asian tribes. Jahangir introduced the use of marble in the construction of water channels, fountains, and roofed pavilions. Shah Jahan revealed an intense desire for symmetry and passion for ornamentation, which is apparent in the intricate detail of the gardens at the Taj Mahal and the palace garden within the walls of the Red Fort at Shahjahanabad. He elevated marble to the status of a supreme construction material, and achieved a truly breathtaking blend of palace and garden.

Babur (1508-1530)

The story of the Mughal gardens then begins with Babur, a born naturalist who was attuned to every nuance of nature. Nostalgic for the cool breezes and temperate climate of Ferghana, he was nevertheless enchanted with the cycle of seasons in India, and the profusion of flower and

Top : the remains of Babur's garden, Aram Bagh, Agra.
Above : water fountains at Achabal in Kashmir.

fruit. He built several gardens, his favourite of the three attributed to him in India being the Ram Bagh or Aram Bagh (Garden of Rest) also known as Nur-Afshan, on the east bank of the Yamuna at Agra. It was extensively renovated in later years by Nur Jahan, Jahangir's wife. Babur ordered the swampy and irregular bank reinforced by a massive masonry wall along the edge of the river, and heavy stones and earth were used to build the foundations of a high riverfront terrace with geometrically laid out elevated walkways. At the south of the site, a fine aquaduct and octagonal well provided water through hollow courses which derive obviously from Persian irrigation.

Gardeners were brought from Persia to tend these gardens and to train local workers, and apart from the tamarind and citrus trees so common to Hindustan, new varieties of fruit and unusual flowers were cultivated in orderly beds and groves.

Babur's nobles were eager to follow their king's example; and the east bank of the Yamuna flowered with luxuriant *char-baghs*. At Nur-Afshan, Babur held court under the silken awnings of the raised stone *chabutras,* and he is said to have been buried here for a while before his body was taken to Kabul.

Humayun (1530-1556)

Unlike his father, Humayun's appreciation of the fine arts was not matched by similar skills in battle, and he spent the better part of his reign fleeing from place to place. Consequently, though he languished in many a garden, he never built any of repute. Ironically, it was his tomb at Delhi built by his widow Haji Begum that served as the model of the tomb-garden in India, and is possibly the only one to survive without any alteration. The stone walls of the *char-bagh* enclose 30 acres of land. Four wide causeways lead to the central tomb of red sandstone and marble, which rises on its high platform like the ancient cosmic mountain. Thus, symbolically, the tomb-garden justified the idea of unity between the mortal and the immortal world. The central pavilion of tomb-gardens became the mausoleum, and the site was looked after by holy men.

The area is repeatedly divided by minor water courses into a total of 32 plots. The cut limestone water channels are shallow in depth, and minute differences in levels create a constant ripple of water.

Tomb-gardens were entered through a large entrance gateway and forecourt. The gateway provided quarters for religious staff and caretakers, and the orchards contained within this court provided income for the tomb's maintenance.

Akbar (1556-1605)

The greatest of the Mughals was an empire builder *par excellence,* a mystic and a humanist. Although he was more inclined to matters of governance than to mere artistic pursuits, it was nevertheless under his rule that some of the finest palace gardens were built in Agra, Fatehpur Sikri and Kashmir. The shores of the Dal Lake in Srinagar were bejewelled with Mughal gardens which, by the end of Jahangir's reign, are said to have totalled over 700.

Akbar's main contribution to garden architecture was the Hari Parbat and Nasim Bagh in Srinagar. The former is a fortress which contained a small temple, courtyard and a water garden. A canal links the fortress with Dal Lake and on its western bank lies Nasim Bagh, the Garden of Breezes. This was the earliest of the Mughal gardens in

Top : Pinjaur Gardens at the foot of the Himalayas.
Above : the presence of a natural spring gave rise to the garden of Verinag.

Kashmir to be used as a summer house and both Shah Jahan and Jahangir nurtured it lovingly in their time.

A perfect example of geometrical precision is Akbar's tomb at Sikandra. Begun in his lifetime it was completed by Jahangir and bears the inscription:

"These are the gardens of Eden, enter them to live forever."

The *tour de force* at Sikandra is the five-storeyed tomb, "a maze of staircases, terraces and cupolas", built exactly in the centre of a walled enclosure. Four identical, wide, raised causeways lead to four gateways, the main entrance being from the south. Water along the causeway is supplied by four main tanks set in the raised platform, while a second line of tanks is placed further down each causeway. Akbar's cenotaph is in marble and placed on the topmost storey exactly above the actual tomb. The architecture of this monument is so strong that without its dense tree cover, which must have once existed, the building with its four lower storeys in sandstone would have overpowered the landscape.

Jahangir (1605-1627)

Like his great grandfather, Jahangir was passionately interested in plants and flowers and it was he and his talented wife Nur Jahan who transformed Kashmir into a veritable garden of paradise. He visited Kashmir time and again and a number of *sarais* and small resting places were built along the way. But of all his garden resorts, Shalimar Bagh is unique. A terraced *char-bagh*, it is approached by boat via a canal with fields on either side. The place is entirely secluded and has an air of repose. Building and landscape are in perfect accord with one another here.

163

Above : Nishat Bagh is said to be the most spectacular of the Kashmir gardens. Opposite page : water was an important aspect of the paradise garden, as seen here at Shalimar.

The focus of attention is the Black Pavilion meant for the *zenana*, the ladies of the court, the central point from where four vistas open. On the terrace below is the Diwan-e-Am or the Hall of Public Audience with its black marble water throne built atop the central water course. A small cascade of water fell into the lowest pool which must eventually have led to the canal. As the water flowed into a tank at the lowest level, coloured lights twinkled in *chini khanas* (pigeon holes) made in the sides of the terrace. Shalimar owes its beauty to both Jahangir who chose the site and to Shah Jahan who helped him with the design and later developed it.

The presence of natural springs gave rise to the gardens at Achabal and Verinag, both being places of worship as well. Both sites are dominated by an imposing backdrop of mountains and at Achabal the abundance of water is apparent as it flows and sparkles in the sun before rushing over a climatic waterfall. Here, two small summer houses and pavilions, and stone terraces were built by Nur Jahan.

At Verinag, said to be the source of the river Jhelum, the spring is enclosed in an octagonal tank with arcaded recesses around it. The original palace has disappeared but what remains of its design depicts a simple octagon and the canal which disappears into the background hills.

The most spectacular of Kashmir's gardens is Nishat Bagh said to be created by Asaf Khan, Nur Jahan's brother. It is on a grand scale, rising from the lake in a dramatic series of twelve terraces representing the twelve signs of the Zodiac. A pink roofed pavilion opens out into a scene of astonishing beauty across the tranquil lake. This was not a royal garden, so there were only two divisions, the pleasure garden and the *zenana* terrace garden. The central water course, dotted with tiny fountains, rippled through a series of reflecting pools. Stone and marble seats were placed at vantage points emphasizing the change in levels. Architecturally the walls of the three-storeyed *zenana* terrace stand out with their wide arches, balconied openings and gazebos at either end. The turret must have been a favourite place for the cloistered ladies from where they could look out on the outside world.

The tomb of Itmadudaullah, Nur Jahan's memorial to her father, is noted more for its architectural qualities than for its landscaping which was based on an under-

ground system of pipes supplying water to the grounds around the central mausoleum. The exquisite *pietra dura* work distinguishes it as one of the most feminine and ornate garden tombs. The remaining gardens ascribed to Jahangir's reign include Khusrau Bhagh in Allahabad, a terraced tomb-garden where Jahangir's son Khusrau lies buried with his mother and sons.

Shah Jahan (1628–1656)

The high point of the building arts under the Mughals was reached during the reign of Shah Jahan. Orthodox, yet sensitive to cultural pursuits, he invited a number of Indian and foreign artists and craftsmen to execute his grand designs. Persian influence returned to building, and with it a formality which sat well with the ambience of the level plains where he preferred to live. White polished marble was introduced, which was used to perfection in the Taj Mahal. Two significant gardens in Kashmir, the Chasma Shahi (said to have been built by Mardan Khan, a governor of Kashmir), and the Char Chinar were Shah Jahan's contribution to this mountain region.

Chasma Shahi nestles at the foot of the mountains and is fed by a powerful spring. It is a miniature garden with two pavilions at different levels. Water ripples down a steep patterned surface into a square pool from the main pavilion, which is Kashmiri in character. An arched gateway at the entrance, which looks out into the valley, leads to an extensive flower garden which steps up to the second level.

Char Chinar rests on the lake island of Sona Lank, a place purely for delight, whose four corners were each planted by Shah Jahan with a *chinar* tree so typical of Kashmir. The garden is barely visible except for the deep shadow of the *chinar* trees in the lake.

It is not possible here to describe in detail all of the gardens laid out in Shah Jahan's reign, either by his wives or governors, so one can only emphasize the magnitude of building activity in the emperor's time by listing them: Shalimar Bagh in Delhi, Shalimar Bagh in Lahore, the Lahore Fort, the Agra Fort, the Red Fort in Delhi, and finally the most magnificent of them all, the Taj Mahal. Terracing, flower parterres, water jets, cascades spraying water over *chini khanas* and carved pavilions were common to all in varying degrees of complexity and details. In the Red Fort, apart from the gardens which stretched beyond the moat along Chandni Chowk, the grounds of the Fort contained two major landscaped areas. The Hayat Baksh or Life Giving Garden, whose northern and southern ends were marked by the Sawan and the Bhadon pavilions (Sawan and Bhadon are the seasons corresponding with the rainy months of July and August) was where ladies enjoyed the monsoon breezes. Along the fortress wall facing the river there was a terrace, at the end of which was a pavilion. Some idea of the grandeur and wealth of Shah Jahan's time can be estimated by the description of details in these gardens: 49 fountains were in one central pool while 112 existed on the sides, each of which was silverplated. In the arch shaped niches below the waterfalls, gold and silver pots were placed, containing silver flowers by day and candles by night.

The Agra Fort is known for its Jasmine Tower where Shah Jahan was held prisoner by his son Aurangzeb and from where he could gaze in his last days at the tomb of his beloved wife Mumtaz Mahal. The stately buildings of the Agra Fort remain, but the gardens Manchi Bhawan (Fish Square) and Angoori Bagh (Grape Garden) have withered away.

From the eastern terrace of the Agra Fort one finally

glimpses the Taj Mahal. This is a classical *char-bagh* except that the tomb, instead of being at the centre, is at one end of the garden on a raised platform which abuts the river on one side. This jewel of monuments is offset by two red sandstone buildings at each end of the cross axis, one a mosque and the other an assembly hall. On the river side the retaining wall thrusts into the river so that the monument seems to rise like a mirage out of the water itself. In the centre of the garden a large rectangular tank mirrors the tomb. Star shaped parterres have been preserved along the main canal. Breathtakingly beautiful at all times of the year, in the day or night, from the river or from its entrance gateway, the Taj Mahal was the handiwork of many craftsmen who built and landscaped it and also embedded its silvery walls with glittering jewels. But it was ultimately due to the emperor's own driving force that the Taj Mahal surpassed all other Mughal monuments in purity and perfection, a quality which it owes as much to its surrounding context of river and garden.

Aurangzeb (1658-1707)

Although Aurangzeb's contribution to architecture was considerable, there is only one garden that stands out in his reign. The great tide of landscape arts which had reached its climax with Shah Jahan subsided with his son. The mausoleum of Rabi-e-Daurani at Aurangabad in the Deccan is but a debased replica of the Taj. But the garden of Pinjaur at the foot of the Himalayas which was built by Aurangzeb's foster brother, Fadai Khan, is worth a mention. An ancient garden is said to have existed on this site which was restored by Fadai Khan. The garden is unusual

in that it is entered from a higher level and descends in seven terraces along a central water course. The design is unimaginative and there is no sense of intimacy or enclosure in spite of the protective back-drop of the Himalayan foothills. Aurangzeb in his religious zeal is said to have ostracized even the Hindu craftsmen who fortunately found employment with Rajput royalty, under whose patronage the gardens designed by the Mughals now bloomed.

It is pertinent to consider here that all art forms in those times were exclusively patronized by the court. Unlike the commercial guilds that encouraged commoner participation during the Buddhist and Hindu periods, the appreciation of arts under the Muslims was the prerogative of Royalty, and its degrees of simplicity or opulence depended on the prevailing health of the empire. The Mughal gardens served as imperial *darbars*, sites of royal festivity and merriment, and were places to be lived in, visited or enjoyed only by nobility and members of the royal family.

Today Mughal gardens have either disappeared or run dry or been built upon. There is an air of desolation where nature or man have not been generous in nurturing them. Yet, although the water channels have dried up and the cypress avenues are nonexistent, although bushes grow carelessly wild and untended, the sudden fragrance of jasmine or the pungent whiff of an orange tree, a bunch of water lilies in a lone monsoon pool, and sometimes in the early morning the call of peacocks, can bring to life the vision of these gardens of paradise in all the splendour of their royal existence.

165

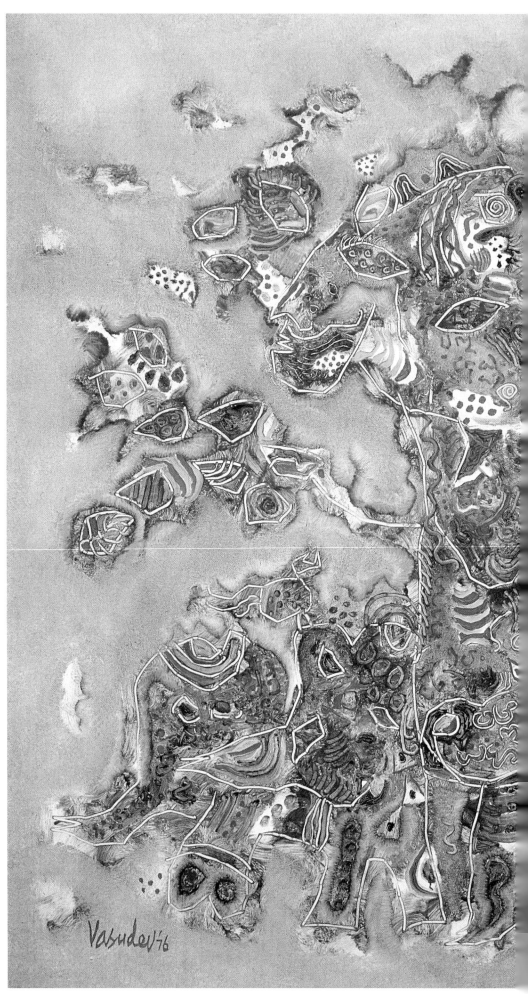

Contemporary painting by S.G. Vasudev entitled "Kalpanika-II". Courtesy National Gallery of Modern Art, New Delhi.

166

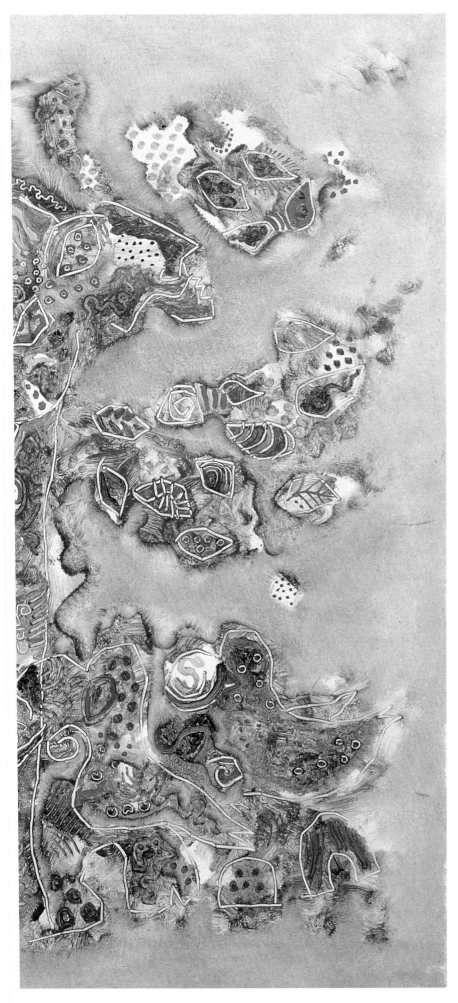

Images on a dewdrop

KRISHNA CHAITANYA

This is not a scholarly essay on the *haiku* for which task I would in any case be not competent. Most of my knowledge of it has been gained through translations and there is loss even in the best of transcreations. But, during a two-month sojourn in Japan, I have been introduced to the music too of the *haiku,* without the steady beat of rhyme, but rich in delicate assonances, flute-notes so low and velvety in pitch as to be no more than whispered intimations. And I have seen how these exquisite miniature poems—three short lines and a total syllable count of seventeen—are most characteristic of the Japanese sensibility which has perfected the artistry for extended reveries using extremely finite space. In the form of the dwarf pine created by the Bonzai horticultural technique, I saw a giant tree which has stood on a headland for decades and weathered a hundred storms. In the upper garden of Seihoji, I heard the torrent and saw its emerald' water, though there was no water, only green moss on the dry bed. In the Zen gardens of Ryonji and Daitokuji, the spreads of gravel and a few rocks in the small temple courtyard, gave the illusion of vast panoramas of earth and sea, islands and mountains. The *haiku* holds the same power of transfiguration.

I still have not disclosed why I ventured on a mention of the *haiku.* The butterfly is seen to flutter through poem after miniature poem, linking garden and wood, hill and dale, with gossamer threads of association. Perhaps the *haiku* itself, as light-winged as the butterfly, can be used to spin silken threads to link Japan and India, lands far apart geographically, but which have already drawn close to each other over the centuries through many cultural associations.

The *Kokinshu,* the anthology compiled by Emperor Daigo in the early tenth century, consists mostly of the *tanka,* an earlier form which is slightly longer, with five lines and thirtyone syllables. But what his aide Tsurayuki said in the preface applies equally to the *haiku.*

"The poetry of Japan, as a seed, springs from the heart of man creating countless leaves of language. And so the heart of man came to find expression in words for his joy in the beauty of blossoms, his wonder at the song of birds, and his tender welcome of the mists that bathe the landscape, as well as his mournful sympathy with the evanescent dew."

Joy in the beauty of the world, and sadness at its evanescence, are both mentioned here; the stress is perhaps a shade on the latter, for Tsurayuki goes on to mention the poets

"gazing upon the mirror's doleful reflections of the ravages of time or trembling as they watched the ephemeral dewdrop quivering on the beaded grass."

172

The kriti in Karnatak music

SAKUNTALA NARASIMHAN

Opposite page : Saraswati, Goddess of Learning and Music holds the ancient stringed instrument, the veena in her hand. South Indian painting of the Mysore School, 19th century. Courtesy National Gallery of Modern Art, New Delhi. Above : musicians pay homage to the saint-composer Thyagaraja at an annual function at Thiruvaiyaru.

If you visit a family in south India, it is likely that along with a cup of steaming coffee that the south is so famous for, you will also be treated to the strains of music. For music, and even classical music, is very much part of the pattern of everyday life, especially in the south. Along with the music of the north (which is known as Hindustani music), the music of the south (known as Karnatak music) shares some extraordinary characteristics: a very long history, stretching over some 3,000 years, for one thing; an extraordinary variety in rhythm patterns and melodic scales, for another; and a peculiar manner of embellishing the notes with curves and frills known as *gamakas* which give the music a characteristic oriental flavour. Karnatak music in particular has one additional extraordinary feature: the constant presence of classical music as part of the daily life of the people. As part of her daily prayer, a housewife will place fresh flowers before the family deity, light a wick lamp and sing a song known as a *kirtana* or *kriti*. This same *kriti* can also be heard on a concert platform during a formal recital by a professional artiste.

In temple rituals and in weddings, a naming ceremony or a housewarming, or any auspicious observance, the air

Above : metal image of the saint-composer Annamacharya, the creator of the kriti *as we know it today. Opposite page : the sublime devotion of the* kriti : *eminent Karnatak singer M.S. Subbulakshmi.*

of festivity is enhanced by the *kritis* in classical style played on the *nagaswaram,* a traditional woodwind instrument.

All through history, music and religion have gone together in the Indian ethos, woven together like warp and weft. As with other forms of artistic expression, music was considered a means of reaching for god. It was *nadopasana,* seeking the divine through sound. In this ethos, music enriched both listener and the performer through aesthetic experience. It is not surprising, then, that most *kritis* are devotional in content, in praise of one of the deities in the Hindu pantheon. They can also be descriptive or based on a particular episode from mythological lore (like the epic *Ramayana*), or sometimes even erotic in content. It should be noted that, in the Hindu interpretation, the lover pining for her beloved is identified as the individual soul seeking union with God, so that even erotic lyrics assume a deeper and serious interpretation.

A *kriti* composition consists of lyrics, usually in the Sanskrit, Telugu or Tamil language, set to a particular tune and rhythm cycle. It can be very short and simple, no more than three minutes long, or very long and complicated, taking as much as twenty minutes to perform. In general, it has three divisions, a beginning called the *pallavi* which is no more than one or two lines of lyrics; a second section known as *anupallavi,* the music of which takes the notes of the *pallavi* forward and higher up in the scale; and a concluding part called the *charanam,* the second half of which usually repeats the music of the *anupallavi.* In the most common type of *kriti,* the entire composition will be six to eight lines of lyrics, divided into these three sections. Each *kriti* is set to a particular *raga* (melodic mode) and *tala* (rhythm). The *raga* is the seed of melody which the creativity of the artiste brings to full flower. It has its rules of prescribed notes used in defined permutations and combinations. Each different combination of sharp and flat notes will evoke a different musical mode and ambience. The musical idea inherent in the *raga* is unfolded and elaborated by the musician, who has meditated upon and practised all the technical possibilities and emotional colouring it offers. The composer of the lyrics of the *kriti* is also usually the composer of the tune, so that the mood of the lyrical content (joy, supplication or pathos, for instance) matches the mood of the melodic scale employed.

The melodic mood picture outlined by the notes of the *raga* gains its depth and richness through various decorative inflections and curves used in the production of the notes. Technically, these embellishments are known as *gamakas.* Each *raga* has its own *gamakas,* whose proper use must be learned by experience, because no written notation can fully express the subtleties or the shades of the curves. Elaborate rules govern the kinds of *gamakas* called for in each *raga,* graces like tremolo, vibrato, glide and so on. The overall effect is a continuous curve of melody that cannot be analysed into component rules of grammar.

Tala is time measure or rhythm pattern, and the choice of *tala* for a *kriti* will match the metre of the lyrics—a *kriti* set to Mohanam *raga,* one of the popular scales, and set to Rupaka *tala,* for instance, will employ the notes of the pentatonic scale C D E G and B with a time measure of six beats per rhythm cycle.

A vocalist usually marks the rhythm cycle with his hand, using beats and finger counts to denote the points of each cycle. Instrumentalists performing on the *veena* or *gottuvadyam,* two stringed, plucked instruments of

the south, mark the beats on a set of secondary strings, plucked at the appropriate points of the music, with the help of the little finger. In the case of the bamboo flute or the violin, the latter of which was introduced from the West some 200 years ago and has now become a solo instrument of great popularity, the artiste keeps track of the beats either with the help of the percussionist, or intuitively.

There are *kritis* that are set to very easy tunes so that even novices can reproduce them; others are complicated in both melody and rhythm, requiring considerable mastery in performance. In either case, performers memorise the composition and perform without scores.

A *kriti* can be presented on its own, by reproducing what one has learnt from the teacher, or it can be preceded and followed by improvisations based on the musician's own imagination. This latter form is mostly heard on concert stages.

Improvisation has a very important place in Indian music. A musician's skill is judged not only by how faithfully and beautifully he or she performs the set piece (the *kriti* composition) but also the range of the artiste's imagination in spinning out extempore melodic and rhythmic patterns. The more varied the patterns, the more the music is lauded. This improvisation can take the form of

rhythm-free *alapanas* (melody patterns) in the *raga* of the kriti. This *alapana* has no lyrics, and is developed along certain conventional rules. It has, of course, to restrict itself to only those semitones that are permitted in that particular *raga;* it begins usually in slow tempo, in the lower notes and progressively works up to a crescendo in fast speed, in the higher notes. The aim is to show the artiste's command over the grouping of notes and the grammar of the *raga*, his voice culture or finger technique and his aesthetic sensibilities in building up a tonal mood picture of the melody.

After the accompanist gets a chance for a similar improvisation using the same sets of notes, the *kriti* follows, with percussion accompaniment joining in. At an appropriate point, a line of lyrics is again taken up for elaboration, but this time within the rhythmic framework, spinning out the lyrics with extempore variations of the basic tune. This is known as *niraval*. This too will be in slow tempo first and then proceed to faster passages.

A different kind of improvisation is also appended to the *kriti*, usually to the same line of lyrics, immediately following the *niraval*. This is the presentation of extempore solfa patterns called *kalpana swara*, successive sorties being of increasing length and complexity and ending precisely at the point of the rhythm cycle where the line of lyrics

Above : the Trinity of Karnatak music.
Top left : Muthuswami Dikshitar. Top right: Thyagaraja.
Above : Shyama Shastri. Opposite page : Krishna, the
Divine Musician, plays the flute. South Indian painting of
the Mysore School, 19th century. Courtesy Karnataka
Chitrakala Parishath, Bangalore.

begins. Although these are not pre-rehearsed and are spun out on the spur of the moment, yet a seasoned musician will be able to string together very dextrous and exciting phrases, some of them involving intricate rhythmic patterns.

None of these improvisational elements is obligatory. A *kriti* can be, and often is, presented on its own without an *alapana* prelude, and can be enjoyed for its own beauty. Or there may be *alapana* and a *kriti*, without any *swara* improvisations. An *alapana* without a *kriti* following in the same *raga* is not presented. In this sense the *kriti* becomes, indeed, the mainstay of every concert programme. This *alapana* can be very short, or long and elaborate; the whole item built round a *kriti* can thus be no more than three minutes or take the greater part of an hour. A series of such *kriti* items make up a concert recital.

Instrumentalists too perform the same *kritis* as vocalists, though without the lyrics. Although the percussion accompanist in a concert provides only the rhythmic background, he too needs deep knowledge of *kritis* in order to be able to enhance the beauties of the composition with appropriate phrases on his own instrument. The *mridangam,* a two-faced drum hollowed out of wood and held horizontally, is the percussion instrument usually featured. This, along with the violin, is the standard accompaniment in a concert. A second percussionist performing on the *ghatam,* an earthen pot held against the abdomen and played with the fingers of both hands, or the *kanjira* which looks like a tambourine with a piece of skin stretched over a circular frame, is also used in some concerts along with the *mridangam.*

We have seen how music and religion have always been intertwined. Hindu mythology places the *veena,* an ancient Indian stringed instrument, in the hands of Saraswati, the Goddess of Learning and Music. While music in north India was nurtured through the patronage of the royal courts, Karnatak music with its accent on devotion was nurtured through temple patronage. A large number of classical compositions are the spontaneous outpourings of inspired devotees. The Tevaram hymns of the 7th century were composed by poet-saints and even today rank as the priceless heritage of Karnatak music. The *kriti,* too, was born of a similar devotion. The origin of the *kriti* form is traced back to the 15th century when a prolific and saintly composer named Annamacharya (1408-1503) poured forth 32,000 inspired songs in praise of his favourite deity, Lord Venkateswara of Tirupati temple in Andhra Pradesh state. Of these, only about 12,000 verses without music have been discovered in copper plate inscriptions found in a vault of the temple at Tirupati. These are now being re-set to music and propagated. Annamacharya was the first to conceive the *kriti* form in the shape that we know it today with its conventional divisions of *pallavi, anupallavi,* and *charanam.*

The form Annamacharya originated was perfected three hundred years later. There can be no account of Karnatak music and of *kritis* without mentioning the Trinity of Karnatak music, as Thyagaraja (1763-1847), Muthuswami Dikshitar (1775-1835) and Shyama Shastri (1763-1827) are known. They were contemporaries; all three lived in the Tanjore district of Tamil Nadu and all three were saint composers, with supranatural experiences and mystic powers. It is the Trinity's *kritis* that still dominate all concert repertiores even today, more than 150 years after their passing away.

Among the Trinity, Thyagaraja was pre-eminent because of the versatility of his genius. Out of the 700 odd songs

prosody and highly philosophical lyrics. Another speciality of his style is his use of melodies (*ragas*) borrowed from the Hindustani system, reportedly a consequence of his travel to Banaras city in north India.

The third of the Trinity, Shyama Shastri, specialised in a style that was in between the other two, neither as easy-flowing as Thyagaraja's nor as involved as Dikshitar's. All three lived and composed as supreme devotees of the muse, and it would be difficult to visualise a concert that does not rely heavily on their compositions. They in fact became models for all composers after their time. Some of their *kritis* are contemplative, and some full of information (Dikshitar, for instance, catalogues intricate astronomical and astrological details in his famous Navagraha *kriti* on the nine planets); others describe incidents in their lives. Thyagaraja's *kriti* "Nidhichala sukhama" in Kalyani *raga* is said to have been composed when he was invited to sing for royalty, with promises of fabulous gifts. Thyagaraja spurned the invitation, declaring, through the song, that no gift could match the pleasure of singing Rama's praise. Yet others describe incidents from the *Ramayana* or the *Puranas*, the sacred texts in Sanskrit dating dack to the pre-Christian era. In each composition, poetry and melody enhance each other to make an extraordinary and creative crystallisation of poetic excellence, musical aesthetics and technical virtuosity.

Many other composers of *kritis* have added to our heritage, among them a royal scion of the erstwhile state of Travancore in what is now Kerala state. Maharaja Swati Tirunal was not only a ruler and patron of fine arts, but a versatile scholar well-versed in several languages. Within his short life span of 34 years, he composed several *kritis* in Sanskrit, Malayalam and even Hindustani. He was a contemporary of the Trinity. *Kriti* compositions have been handed down from generation to generation, from teacher to disciple, entirely through the oral tradition, and are committed to memory. Notation is a recent 20th century development in Karnatak music, and even now, it can present at best only the bare framework of the tune of the composition. This is because it is necessary to add curves and embellishments (*gamakas*) to the notes to beautify the rendering and infuse it with emotion, according to the canons of aesthetics. These nuances cannot be conveyed through notation, however elaborate. They can only be learned through the ear. The absence of written records is one reason why many compositions of earlier centuries are now lost to us.

In recent decades, *kritis* in the Tamil language have also become popular, because it is a language understood and spoken by a large section of the south Indian population. The Tamil *kritis* of Papanasam Sivan, for instance, have become almost as popular as those of the Trinity.

There are other forms of compositions too, included in concerts, *javali* and *tillana*, for example; the former is a light classical song with erotic themes while the *tillana* highlights rhythm patterns with very little lyrics. There is also the item known as the *pallavi* which is an entirely improvised elaborate rendering of a single line of lyrics. However, the *kriti* still holds pride of place and is in fact so versatile that it has been incorporated into recitals of classical dance too.

The *kriti* form that Annamacharya fashioned 500 years ago still thrives as a quintessential musical expression, and a vehicle for spiritual, intellectual as well as artistic endeavour for both composer and performer. In this sense, it marks a watershed in the history of Karnatak music, and the beginning of the period of our musical history for which proper chronicles are available.

of his that are preserved, some are so simple that a child could learn them, and some are so complicated that performing them competently becomes a test of a musician as a seasoned artiste. His famous *pancharatnas*, a composite set of five songs in five traditional *ragas*, are among the longest *kritis* in existence. His genius spans a very wide melodic range, from the most popular to relatively obscure and difficult *ragas*. His rhythm patterns are simple, but can also be complicated gaits and off beat arrangements that test one's sense of rhythm. Some of his compositions even incorporate folk tunes and lullabies, turning them into a classical mould and investing them with melodic beauty. His compositions are the rapturous outpourings of a devotee who had dedicated himself body and soul to singing in praise of his deity Rama.

Besides taking the *kriti* form to the pinnacle of formalised beauty and exploring its myriad musical possibilities, Thyagaraja also devised decorative elements within the composition to embellish each line. These technical embellishments, known as *sangatis,* are step-by-step melodic variations of the basic musical arrangement of a line of lyric, starting with the simplest and going on to the most complicated; these are pre-set and not extempore variations. This is unlike the *niraval*, which resembles the *sangati,* but is an on-the-spot improvisation of the melodic line developed by the performer. Some Thyagaraja *kritis* are famous for their astounding number of *sangatis* for a single line, running at a time to a dozen or more. Thyagaraja's death anniversary in January is observed every year at Thiruvaiyaru in Tanjore district when musicians known and unknown gather to pay homage through recitals of his compositions.

Thyagaraja's songs were lyrical and spontaneous, and mostly in easy-to-understand, almost conversational Telugu. Dikshitar's, on the other hand, were more scholarly, and were in Sanskrit, which was not a spoken language. Dikshitar's *kritis* abound in metric grandeur,

Himalaya: our fragile heritage

N. D. JAYAL

The world's loftiest and most majestic mountain chain, the Himalaya, is the global heritage of all mankind. The sublime quality of this 'Abode of Snows' has, from the beginning of time, inspired the sages and saints of India in their ancient texts and scriptures to bestow the stamp of divinity on its snow-clad peaks and icy glaciers, life-sustaining rivers and lush valleys. Places of pilgrimage were established to which, braving hazards of climate and terrain, devotees from every corner of the country have flocked to seek salvation. But now the Himalaya are also a powerful magnet for those who come in ever-increasing numbers from all over the world in search of adventure and challenges unmatched elsewhere. The process of 'modernisation' and 'development' has in recent times opened up the Himalaya's sensitive and cloistered environment to rapid flux, with consequences that are often unpredictable. Nature's balance is inevitably strained, while we strive to grasp its mysteries, and understand its origins.

The Himalaya is, geologically speaking, a young and still growing mountain range. Sixty million years ago a plate of the earth's crust carrying the Indian land-mass travelled 5000 kms. from near the South Pole and collided with Laurasia, thus heaving up the Himalaya. The most substantial rise took place in the past 38 million years and

Above : spectacular shot of Himalaya, the world's loftiest and most majestic mountain chain. Top right : young children in the Spiti Valley.

the final thrust upward has occurred in the past one million years. The tectonic forces that brought the Himalaya into being also created an extraordinarily complex environment, exercising a very powerful influence upon the entire subcontinent. The mountain ranges are the major factor in determining the climate of India, holding in the beneficent monsoon rains and affording protection in winter from the cold Siberian winds. They also produce their own climate, ranging from near-polar in the higher reaches to tropical humid in the foothills of the eastern segment. The winter snows are stored by the Himalaya for feeding the perennial northern rivers. The climate and geologic variety have contributed towards the creation of diverse ecosystems ranging from the cold desert of Ladakh to the tropical rainforests of Arunachal Pradesh, and encompassing an enormous wealth of natural living and non-living resources. Through their altitudinal zones, the latitudinal gradation from the equator to the poles are recaptured over short vertical distances. The sharp zoning in vegetation, and consequently animal life, results in extreme diversity of plants and animals. Lush tropical rainforests to timber-line and alpine meadows can be traversed in vertical heights of less than three thousand metres. Their complex assay of ridges and valleys multiplies the surface area contained within narrow geographic reaches, and provides conditions equivalent to an archipelago of islands scattered over the sea. Tropical swampy forests, deciduous forests, coniferous forests, rhododendron forests, alpine meadows and often cold as well as hot deserts occur from the *terai* to the snowline within the Himalaya. The rain-shadow effect is pronounced, and even the northern or southern aspects of slopes have a decisive influence over vegetation. The indigenous human communities have evolved rich cultures, adapting themselves to often hostile environment with remarkable vigour and resilience. Such an immense variety of resources are the greatest, and also the most vulnerable, asset of the Himalaya, for this young mountain chain is extremely fragile and highly susceptible to any thoughtless interference in the natural balance of its sensitive ecosystems.

The biological diversity in Himalayan ecosystems co-exists with human cultural diversity. The difficult terrain provides sanctuaries not only for primitive forms of life but also for human civilizations and cultures. They have provided refuge for ancient vegetation types such as the tropical rainforests of north-eastern India and for even the mythical 'Yeti' and his counterparts in other snowy mountains. The Himalaya have in fact served as a highway for living forms to cross its barriers and to also travel along the barrier and spread across its length and breadth. But many such living forms were also stopped from crossing the barrier. The wild sheep and goat are essentially a Eurasian group of animals which moved eastwards along its fringes almost upto South China, while the Malayan squirrel family and the Macaques moved westwards. While the camel and horse groups failed to cross the barrier southwards, the tiger succeeded. For many important plant groups also, the same effects on distribution are noticeable. The Aryans drifted only slowly through the lower passes in the west and pushed the Dravidians southwards, who in turn pushed the Negrito and Austroloid human races farther and farther into forest fastnesses. The Mongolians, however, crossed the Himalaya, and mingling with the North Indian groups, formed the Indo-Mongolians. A melting pot of plants, animals and human groups, the Himalaya have perhaps the richest assemblage of living forms within its

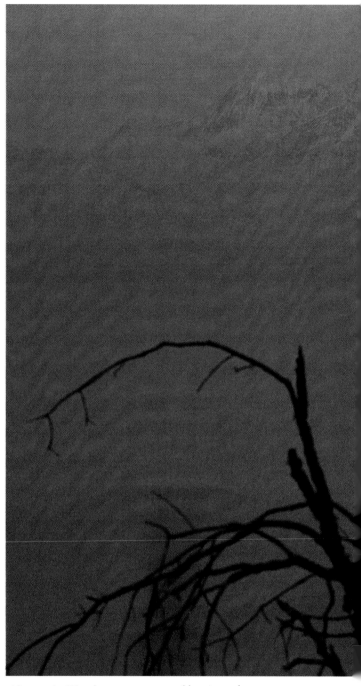

Above : the Himalaya act as a natural barrier and are a major factor in determining the climate of India. Right : the Himalaya contains great human cultural diversity. Monks in Ladakh.

confines—a wealth which is also very fragile.

Life and times have not always been gentle and easy in the demanding environment of these high mountains. Through millennia of slow adaptation, man has learnt to cultivate and raise domesticated animals on the harsh hill slopes. Terrace cultivation, natural gravity irrigation, well adapted cultivated crop varieties, and distinctive life-styles have evolved without undermining the delicate web of the Himalayan mountain ecosystems. Populations were never high and human demands were minimal and well within self-sustaining levels of such ecosystems. Self-reliant, independent and gentle people kept their slow rhythm of life well adapted to the sparse productivity of the high valleys and slopes.

With extension of communications and increasing urbanisation, however, the influx of large numbers of people from outside into the farthest reaches of the Himalaya can easily imperil its sensitive ecosystems. Unadapted to outside processes, the communities and cultures within such ecosystems could lose their identity and quality, or perish altogether. Opening up of moun-

Top : this serene lake in the Central Himalaya is part of a sensitive and cloistered environment. Above : belle from Ladakh. Opposite page : winter in Ladakh : the snow covered fields of Leh.

tains facilitates exploitation of resources, hydro-power, minerals, timber, plants and animal produce to such an extent that greed overtakes and undermines not only the mountains but also the vast plains below. This is the plight of Himalaya today and, with it, the very foundation of human societies in the Gangetic and Brahmaputra Valleys are endangered.

For centuries the natural resources of the Himalaya were utilised by hill communities to meet their basic requirements of food, fuel, fodder, fertiliser, fibre, shelter and water on a sustainable basis and without disrupting nature's balance. Life-styles of such communities evolved in harmony with the surroundings despite the fact that mountains are not the best habitats for man, because their physical constraints reduce their capacity to support large populations. The basic life-support systems of soil, water and biota are limiting factors in mountain ecosystems, obliging hill communities to use their environment and resource frugally and rationally without depleting the resource capital. The soil is fragile because of steep slopes and rapid weathering; the forests are also fragile because the plant communities have delicately adjusted against the harsh environment; the animals are vulnerable because they can survive only within a narrow range of conditions, and the people are fragile because their simple life-styles and isolation have not moulded them to withstand outside pressures.

There were always thus few people in the hills who subsisted on minimum resources from large areas. However, with 'development', waves of people with a new philosophy of life based on the market economy entered the mountains and introduced an exploitative approach which has disrupted the erstwhile delicate balance. Forests were taken away from community ownership and reserved for meeting commercial requirements of timber in the plains; a network of roads was extended into the mountains for exploitation of timber, plant and mineral resources; and gigantic hydro-power schemes to support industries elsewhere were launched. At the same time, the human and domestic animal populations of hill communities also increased, adding to the already heavy pressures on the limited natural resources of the mountains. With the disappearance of vegetation on an extensive scale, water and fuel resources dwindled and soils rapidly lost their productivity. This has led not only to large scale migration of the hill people to the plains for their survival, but also made it impossible for those left behind to survive without great hardship in their desperate search over long distances for fuel and water. This indeed was the genesis of the now famous 'Chipko' movement in the hills, with the realisation by the remnant hill communities, comprising largely of the womenfolk, that their survival depended upon the protection of their life-supporting water and soil resources provided by the forests.

In the last century, the reservation of the best forests by our colonial rulers for commercial use led to conflicts and large scale denudation of the Himalayan forests. The resulting degradation of the delicate mountain ecosystem, and the impoverishment of the people's life-support systems, gave birth to an important grassroots environment movement. The movement dated from the early seventies of this century, and aimed at the protection of forests from depradation. In the Central Himalaya, it is called 'Chipko'. But the roots of this movement extend deeply in India's *aranya* or forest culture, which thrived in the woods. The sages who lived in forest *ashrams* with their students pondered over the problems of mankind, and developed a philosophy which believed in the coexistence

Forests, plants and animals — the Himalaya has the richest assemblage of living forms within its confines — a wealth which is also very fragile.

and interdependence of all forms of life. All creations such as birds, beasts, human beings, rivers and mountains have life; all life is sacred and merits worship; and austerity and wisdom are worthy of respect. This cultural legacy was gradually supplanted, under the impact of colonial rule, by materialistic values. The policy of reservation and commercial exploitation of Himalayan forests was resisted earlier in the century by the people of Uttarakhand and, as a patch-work settlement, *panchayat* or community forests were created. After Independence, the hill people pledged to revive the friendly relationship between the forests and forest-dwellers, now disturbed by commercialisation. They sought an end to exploitation, suggesting instead people's forest labour cooperatives, to ensure availability of raw material for local forest-based small industries. Their aim was a revision of forest settlement. The change in land-use pattern brought about by substituting mixed natural forests by monoculture pine plantations led to accelerated soil erosion. This, coupled with a rapid increase of population, forced a majority of able-bodied men to seek employment in cities in the plains. The main burden of managing the family and caring for the aged, the children and cattle, and carrying on agricultural operations thus fell on the shoulders of the

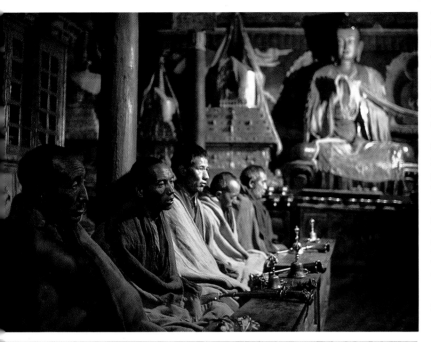

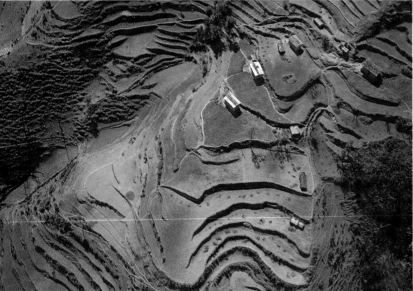

Top : The culture and lifestyle of the Himalayan peoples has evolved over centuries and needs protection from sudden change. Above : dramatic shot of hills gradually stripped of forest cover. Opposite page. Neelkanth peak, Garhwal Himalaya.

womenfolk. They walk long distances to collect such basic necessities of life as water, fuel and fodder, rendered scarce by the loss of tree cover. Under the inspiration of various disciples of Gandhiji and Sarvodaya workers, the process of educating the masses through folk songs, foot-marches, and so on began, and the following slogan was popularised: "What do the forests bear? Soil, water and pure air. Soil, water and pure air, are the basis of life." Women were thus in the forefront of a movement for survival that rapidly spread in the villages to establish the right of the local people over the Himalayan forest resources. The method devised to stop the felling of trees was essentially a non-violent one. It consisted of volunteers, mainly women, embracing or hugging tree trunks in such a manner that woodmen were prevented from plying their axes for fear of injuring the volunteers. In Hindi 'Chipko' means 'to stick to', or 'to embrace', and this is quite literally what the volunteers did—they clung to the trees to stop them from being cut down. Such actions had taken place in four different sites by 1974. Demonstrations against auctioning the forests were organised in 1977. The women of Advani village in Tehri Garhwal tied sacred threads round the trees marked for felling, and declared their firm determination to save the trees even at the cost of their lives. Eventually the state government was compelled to impose a moratorium on felling of trees in areas exceeding 1000 mts. altitude and 30 degrees slope.

The Chipko movement has provided an alternative plan of development in the Himalaya by emphasising that the main products of the forests are soil, water and oxygen, which are all vital for human survival. There was, therefore, urgent need for practising austerity in the use of forest products that need felling of trees, through the use of biogas and solar energy for cooking and by re-cycling of paper. The hope for the future lay in reafforestation through the villagers' own efforts rather than through state ownership and action, as the people were in the best position to protect and plant trees that fulfil their own basic needs of oxygen, water, food, fodder, fuel, fertiliser, fibre and small timber. The Chipko movement realised that to swim against the tide, small groups of humanitarians, scientists, social activists and compassionate literary men were needed. Chipko's search for a strategy for survival has indeed global implications. What Chipko is trying to conserve is not merely local forest resources but the entire life-support system, and with it the option for human survival. Gandhi's mobilization for a new society, where neither man nor nature is exploited and destroyed, sowed the seeds of this civilizational response to a threat to human survival.

Another dimension to the pressures of developmental activities mentioned above was introduced by tourism and mountaineering, rapidly gaining popularity during the short summer months. Foreigners were allowed access to many hitherto prohibited areas, and streams of expeditions to a number of popular peaks led to serious depletion of the limited biological wealth during the crucial growth period in the few summer months. The ingress of scores of large expeditions each year into the Nanda Devi Sanctuary is a classic example of rapid resource depletion of a unique marvel of nature's mountain architecture, where scores of endemic species have evolved under natural protection for a millenia. The slow growth of the plants can be judged from the fact that at high altitudes the birch tree attains a diameter of two centimetres in six years while a juniper bush takes twenty years for the same growth. To save such priceless heritage areas from

destruction, it became inevitable to extend them protection in order to facilitate the slow process of restoration of their biological and natural assets. In these circumstances, national natural heritage areas such as Nanda Devi Sanctuary and the Valley of Flowers have been accorded total protection from all forms of human interference, except for purely scientific work, and have been set aside as National Parks or Biosphere Reserves.

Mountains must be our refuge for contemplation and recreation, and for many societies their very survival depends on them. But before irretrievable damage is done, we must carefully assess to what limits the system can be exploited or developed. We have seen that even non-consumptive exploitation such as tourism or mountaineering can cause havoc unless planned with meticulous care and consideration for the fragility of the ecosystem. The Himalaya are also a sensitive international border, subject to deployment of people requiring a network of strategic roads which should not be constructed thoughtlessly and destructively. The ecological hazards of constructing major dams in the Himalaya and their environmental implications should be fully realized. It is clear that a massive rehabilitation programme is urgently needed to save the Himalaya from serious ecological degradation. A comprehensive resource survey, and planned integrated development with river catchment areas as units, keeping long range perspectives in view, are the key elements for restoring the complex Himalayan ecosystems.

The Himalaya, the world's youngest and highest mountains, are unique in many other aspects. This mountain range, arranged in three distinct folds, links up three very diverse biological regions of the world—the very rich Malayan tropical biogeographic region, the cold temperate Eurasia and the monsoon Indian peninsula. There is in fact a very attenuated connection even with the African-Arabian region. Plants and animals have found a haven in very valuable niches of the Himalaya which now need to be identified and protected as biosphere reserves—an international network of protected areas with representative examples of landscapes, each with its characteristic floral, faunal and human uses where evolution of life can continue in its totality in natural habitats. Areas capable of exploitation for various uses need to be identified and the carrying capacity of each area assessed within a comprehensive management plan. Mass influx of visitors to popular areas will need to be controlled by reducing access and amenities to conform to carrying capacities. Detailed land evaluation surveys and land capability classification are, therefore, an essential prerequisite for avoiding the kind of mistakes which can only be corrected subsequently at great cost.

Any programme for managing and developing our mountain areas should always consider the delicate cultural balance the hill people have evolved to survive in their often very harsh environment. It is easy to destroy this balance by the large scale advent of modern plains cultures and values which are often brazenly exploitative. The denudation of the Central Himalaya has already created disturbing sociological problems leading to emigration and to eco-disasters in adjacent areas. For the hill peoples, very carefully drawn up plans of direct relevance to them need to be implemented, to buffer them against cultural shocks and ease the pressure on their largely subsistence-level existence. Schumacher's concept of "small is beautiful" epitomises the approach to development of our fragile mountains and their sequestered inhabitants which must carefully set aside projects of great eco-destructive potential.

Above : Raghubir Yadav as "Massey Sahib" in the film by Pradeep Krishan. Top right : a tense moment from the film "Paroma". Right : a scene from the film "Manthan" by Shyam Benegal.

196

mafia don, or bandit became "heroes" in the seventies and eighties. It was a reaction—simplistic, no doubt—to the increasingly uncertain political and economic conditions in the country. This kind of film proved a magnet and drew audiences away from the more subtle nuances of the New Cinema. The television serial proved another threat, with its consumerism and advertising.

Currently, the New Cinema is meeting these challenges in a variety of ways. Firstly, some of the New Cinema films are being premiered on television, thus gaining large audiences. Secondly, and more promisingly, enterprising younger directors are evolving forms of expression which will do justice to their themes and concerns without alienating mass audiences.

"New Cinema", or "New Wave Cinema" is not a monolith. Nor can it be conveniently divided into schools or genres without distorting the total picture. And so we shall take up for discussion prominent directors (whether new or established) who have done important work in the last three years.

Let's look first at the younger directors.

To me the most original, the most promising, among the younger directors is Ketan Mehta. His first film, made in the early eighties, was "Bhavni Bhavai". It utilised a popular music and dance form of Gujarat to portray the sufferings and exploitation of the lower castes in times past and present. The film was described by the director as a homage to Bertolt Brecht. Mehta used folk music, dance, rhythm and undercut it with fierce satire. The film is told in the form of a fable of an eccentric King (Naseeruddin Shah) whose son is "lost" to the lower caste. Later the son (in love with a Harijan girl played by Smita Patil) revolts against the king. The film provides two endings—a "humanistic-happy" ending where the kind embraces the lost son, and a brutal one where the son goes to his death to redeem his chosen tribe. The pulsating vigour which marked this film became a regular feature of Mehta's cinematic manner.

Mehta's next film "Holi" (1984) dealt with student unrest on college campuses. "Holi" is a powerful film but perhaps a one-sided one. The form of the film becomes that of a long ballet-opera with musical and dance compositions heightening the theme. The students rise in revolt against bad teaching, bad conditions of living, bad ethos. But their revolt itself is poisoned by their environment and ends in tragedy.

"Mirch Masala" (1985) is Mehta's most ambitious film. Here again the form is epic. Set in the days before Independence, the content is a struggle between a lustful Revenue Collector who is a hireling of the British (Naseeruddin Shah) and a young woman who refuses to surrender to his amorous advances. The form is that of the Hollywood "Western" but it is fused with traditional Indian music and dance. "Mirch Masala" deals with a time when "classical" music had not been divorced from the people. "Mirch Masala" was one of the few "New" films to be a box-office success. It was made in a popular cinema format but its theme and concern—the possibility of a *moral* mass struggle inspired by individual heroism—were genuinely new. New too is the awareness that 'leftist' movements also need heroes. "Mirch Masala" shows a new way to "new cinema". New Cinema can attract mass audiences without losing its soul or compromising its content.

As vibrant a film-maker as Ketan Mehta is the Bengali director Gautam Ghosh, whose "Paar" (1984) has been internationally acclaimed. "Paar" is the story of a husband and wife (Naseeruddin Shah and Shabana Azmi) who are

Above : Shabana Azmi in "Susman." Opposite page top : Goa in the early '60's; scene from Shyam Benegal's "Trikal". Opposite page bottom : the late Smita Patil in Kumar Shahani's "Tarang". To the left is Kanwal Gadhioke.

uprooted as peasants in Bihar by upper caste landlords. They emigrate to Calcutta and go through unbearable misery. At last they get a job to ferry pigs across the river. The struggle to do this becomes an epic one—a kind of intense, tightened-up "Lower Depths". They succeed and survive—at least at a biological level. In the terms of the film, even that becomes a triumph. "Paar" is a film that satisfies the standards of good cinema and remains accessible to the masses.

Another such film is Ramesh Sharma's "New Delhi Times" (1985) which is both a thriller and social expose. Brilliantly shot in Delhi by Subrato Mitra (the former cinematographer of Satyajit Ray), it is a tale of an extremely complicated and twisted political game in the capital city. Here an idealistic editor of a newspaper is used by a politician for his nefarious purposes. The atmosphere of the capital with its high degree of both culture and manipulation, is powerfully captured.

Another interesting young film-maker from whom much is expected is Vidhu Vinod. He made an ostensibly Hitchcock-like thriller in "Khamosh" (1986). It was the story of a typical commercial film unit on location whose shooting schedule is disrupted by a series of strange murders. Vinod uses this story as a framework to mount an attack on commercial cinema both as an expression of corrupt social forces and as a source of further corruption. There is a parody of a rape scene—the principal stock-in-trade of commercial cinema—that is savage in its exposure. Vinod is now making a gangster movie "Parinda" with similar aims in view. In an interview he said: "I have taken the pillars of popular Hindi Cinema and built the whole edifice on them. Then, one by one, I have removed the pillars, hoping that the edifice won't collapse. I want to make a film that will make good cinema proud yet reach the masses and be popular."

There are three other young directors who have done promising work. Prakash Jha started on a light note with "Hip Hip Hurray" (1984), a story of a high-spirited young teacher sent to pull together a public school which is falling apart. He followed this up with the award-winning "Damul" (1985). Jha is an adventurer with camera and compositions and, like most adventurers, he stumbles quite a few times. "Damul" is about corruption at grassroots level in his native state, Bihar. The corruption is political, economic, sexual. There is rivalry among the higher castes and the victims are Harijans and women. Jha gets so involved with camera effect, compositions and lighting that the impact of the film is diluted. Yet "Damul", despite its flaws, has a youthful zest which makes it attractive.

Jha's latest "Parinati" (1987) is even more grim. A tale of destroying greed, it is set and shot marvellously in the Rajasthan desert. It has a kind of medieval malevolence which is gripping. The film recounts the tale of a poor couple put in charge of a religious rest house constructed in the desert for merchants and pilgrims. Out of need, as an insurance against old age, they begin murdering and robbing their visitors and it becomes a destructive habit. A powerful parable for the times.

Jahnu Barua is a young Assamese director (perhaps the only one in this category) who has made three films in the eighties. "Papori" (1986), his second film, is a record of the nightmare of a woman from Assam in north east India who gets caught up in the political crossfire of the state in 1983 during the confrontation between the state and the student's Union. The film powerfully depicts how in today's India there can be no bystanders—every one is trapped into being a participant.

Pradip Kishen's "Massey Saheb" (1986) is something of an oddity in the works of New Cinema. Set in pre-independence India, it goes back to the late twenties but it is not directly about the oppression of the Indians by the British. Instead, it takes up the story of what used to be called a "native Christian", the type who loved to play the go-between connecting British district officials with the "natives".

The film is directly inspired by British writer Joyce Carey's "Mr. Johnson"—a novel which is about an unreliable but charming half-caste in British Africa in the twenties. Joyce Carey's book subtly traced the moral responsibility of the British in creating a half-caste culture which neither belonged to "white" nor "black". Carey's novel has a very direct placing in the heart of African culture. Kishen's difficulty is that in an Indian setting both the native Christian and the white officer represent marginalised cultures. One can laugh at the Christian Massey, but one does not quite believe in him. All the same Kishen's is an interesting effort rendered memorable by the magnificent performance of the central character played by Raghubir Yadav.

If one were to attempt general observations on the younger directors of the mid-eighties, two patterns come to light. Firstly, caste, communal and class divisions are today both sharper and more confused than at any time in India's history. This is partly caused by the increasing modernisation and the accompanying corruption which cuts across all divisions. Film-makers struggle with these

Bodhidharma facing the wall, by Sesshu Toyo (1420-1506).
Ink and light colours on paper.

inchoate processes and attempt to convey their meaning and significance according to their individual understanding and vision. Secondly, the other problem is that of cinematic language, which must be subtle enough to capture the many sided and changing reality and also acceptable enough and easy to understand for the common man.

The established directors have done some remarkable work during the last three years which deserves attention.

Shyam Benegal has made two films "Trikal" (1985) and "Susman" (1986) which explore very different dimensions. "Trikal" is set in the Goa of the early sixties, before its merger with India. It is not merely a record of a fossilized colonial society but also a play with memory and time. It is this intersection of the historical with the para-historical that gives "Trikal" its charm and significance. "Susman" is about earthy current reality—the plight of so-called co-operative weavers in a village in Andhra Pradesh who are exploited by both bright urban entrepreneurs and local rustics. Here Benegal is on the familiar ground of his earlier films "Ankur" and "Manthan". The film has the likeable quality of subdued realism and extremely moving performances by Om Puri and Shabana Azmi as a poor weaver couple.

Govind Nihalani's "Party" (1984) and "Aaghat" (1985) are again very individualistic explorations. "Party", a not totally successful film, explores the present urban–rural malaise through the device of charting the course of a cocktail party of middle class intellectuals, posers, burnt-out cases and self seekers. This is set in a rather black and white fashion against the heroism of a genuine poet-activist who is tortured and killed by the police while fighting for the rights of oppressed tribals. "Aaghat" is one of the few examinations of the current labour union crisis which pits genuine leftists against union gangsters, the latter being an increasing tribe in India. Both films are marked by a vigorous punchy style whose nearest American equivalent would be Sidney Lumet's.

Aparna Sen's "Paroma" (1985) is the best examination attempted so far of the breakdown of a traditional urban

marriage. Compared to Paul Cox's "My First Wife", it may appear too cautious. Yet this story of a beautiful traditional Calcutta wife falling in love with a young and handsome adventurer hauntingly evokes the bourgeois ethos and its attempt to face this challenge.

Kumar Shahane and Mani Kaul in "Tarang" (1984) and "Mati Manas" (1986) respectively maintain their position as India's leading *avant-gardists*—not in a cliched but in a genuinely significant sense. "Tarang", told in a relatively easy to understand narrative form, is the story of a wealthy industrialist family going to pieces because of its feudalism and inner barrenness, and also because of a robust challenge from the more alive segments of society. It's one of the best shot films of the decade. It is also rich in its array of metaphors and allusions—from Urvashi, the goddess of dawn, to Ophelia. "Mati Manas" is one of the most lyrical films I have seen, a kind of song of homage to Indian clay through the ages, from the earliest pottery down to the magnificent last sequence where the camera rushes down an alley of coloured clay horses in Tamilnadu.

The South Indian director, Aravindan, offered "Chidambaram" in 1985 and "Oridathu" in 1986. "Chidambaram" is a tale of Fall, Repentance and Release in the lush surroundings of a Kerala village. Aravindan's film reminds me of the novels of Francois Mauriac. There is a similar guilt (adultery in this case) and transcendence of the transgression. "Oridathu" is Aravindan's most accessible film. Ostensibly, the tale of "progress", namely, the electrification of a Kerala village, it becomes a savage satire of the "onward march" of modern industrial civilisation.

And so to the man I regard as the doyen of current Indian film-makers, Adoor Gopalakrishnan. His "Mukhamukham" (1984) is in part an examination of the fragmentation of the communist movement in India after the fifties. At a deeper level it speaks of the destruction wrought by the confusion between "image" and "reality". The over-idealisation of a man who was once a communist hero leads to disillusionment and eventually tragedy. Satyajit Ray called this film an "act of courage" because of its unrelenting refusal to make concessions to ordinary watchability. His latest film "Ananthram" (1987) is an even more astonishing achievement. Taking up the story of a gifted but unsure young man, Vijayan, Gopalakrishnan explores time, memory, suppressed sex longings and their transmutation into strange forms, in a manner that is at once comical, haunting and tragic. It's impossible to do justice to "Ananthram" without writing a separate article on this single film. The audience can enjoy it as a gossamer-like romantic fable, the discerning may see it as a foray into the world of a special kind of fantasy.

Even when expressed in fantasy, the cinema of the Indian New Wave reflects the reality of this vast country which is almost continental in size. New Cinema forms only a part of the total output of Indian films, today the largest in the world. Working in different languages, exploring themes and concerns rooted in the milieu of their regions, the directors of India's New Cinema have created a body of work that is multi-faceted and multi-dimensional. Its explorations push in different and exciting directions, but its true test will lie in its ability to communicate with the masses.

Opposite page : scene from Shyam Benegal's "Susman".
Above left : poignant moment from Adoor
Gopalakrishnan's "Mukhamukham". Left : Om Puri,
left, as the politician and Shashi Kapoor, right, as the
idealistic editor in Ramesh Sharma's "New Delhi Times".

Bodhidharma facing the wall, by Sesshu Toyo (1420-1506).
Ink and light colours on paper.

The Myriad-Mile Bridge, school of Shubun of the Shokoku-ji monastery in Kyoto.

Dhyana to Zen

PROF. LOKESH CHANDRA

The word Zen is the youngest descendant of the Sanskrit word *dhyana*, and the Pali word *jhana*, which mean 'contemplation, pondering over, meditation'. Its equivalent in the Rigveda is *dhena* in the sense of 'speech reflecting the inner thoughts of man'. Its ancient Iranian or Avestan equivalent is *daena*, which is a common word in the Gathas, meaning 'inner self of man, revelation, faith, religion'. It survives in modern Persian as *din*, 'religion'. Its derivative in Lithuanian is *daina*, the noblest expression of their mind, written at the morning of their world, with the dew still on them. The Lithuanian *daina* speak of a time when joy walked over the earth. They are unique treasures of the thatched roof of the Lithuanian countryside, heart-stirring in their simplicity and subtlety. Likewise, Zen is the warm reality of the living culture of Japan. Japan was moulded late in the history of planet earth, it is geologically young. So is Zen ever young in its simple artless perspective. It is the beauty of function and line, the beauty of the iron of a tea kettle or of a bamboo stirrer. Zen has transformed the primitive and the savage into an exquisite spiritual flower. Elemental and beyond measure, it has become the ceremonial logic of human relations in Japan. The influence of Zen on Japanese art, taste, attitude and perception has been profound. Its sway on the masters of garden design and archery, of tea ceremony and flower arrangement, of poetry and pottery, of Noh plays and swordsmanship, on architects, painters and sculptors, has been pervasive and powerful. The spirit of Zen is part of the very heart of the Japanese people. Zen is an appreciation of intuition and action, an essence and purity, a love of nature as the direct embodiment of the Absolute.

Zen was carried to China as Dhyana Buddhism by Bodhidharma, the youngest son of a king of Kanchi in South India. Bodhidharma reached China early in the sixth century after long peregrinations. He had an audience with the noted patron of Buddhism, Emperor Liang Wu-ti (502-550) of South China. He pointed out to the Emperor the futility of establishing monasteries, copying *sutras* and supporting monks. The historicity of Bodhidharma has been controversial. The first mention of Kanchi is in "The Record of the Transmission of the Lamp", compiled in 1002. The Ch'an tradition derived from Dhyana Buddhism, says that their doctrine was transmitted by an uninterrupted succession of twentyeight Indian patriarchs: from Mahakashyapa, the disciple of the Buddha, to Bodhidharma who brought it to China. Bodhidharma handed down the doctrine to Hui-K'o (traditional dates: 487-593). From him the doctrine was handed through four other Chinese patriarchs to Huineng (639-716). Bodhidharma finally transmitted the "Seal of Mind" to Hui-K'o, who had cut off his arm to express the deep sincerity of his resolve. In the Kozanji ink

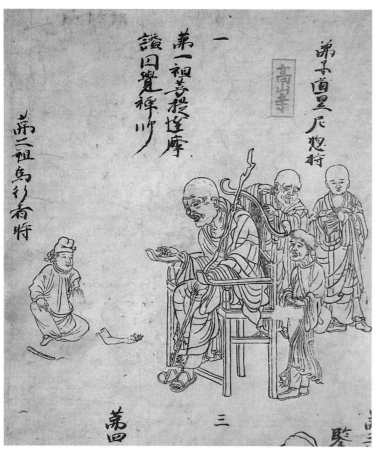

弟子道□□尼惣持

第一祖菩提達摩

諡曰覺禪師

第二祖□□□□

高山寺

Bodhidharma seated on a chair and Hui-K'o the second patriarch seated on the ground. Blood gushes forth from the stump of the latter's cut-off left arm.

scroll of the Six Patriarchs of the Bodhidharma lineage, Hui-K'o kneels down in front of him. Blood gushes forth from the stump of his left arm, and the knife and the cut-off arm lie next to him on the ground. According to late accounts Bodhidharma crossed the Yangtze on a reed, and spent nine years in meditation in front of a rock wall at the Shao-lin monastery.

Bodhidharma had said that of his disciples, Tao-fu had acquired the skin, the nun Tsung-ch'ih the flesh, Tao-yu the bone, but that Hui-K'o had penetrated into the marrow (the essence) of the doctrine. Like this statement, mist surrounds the evolution of the legend of Bodhidharma, which is as controversial as he himself must have been in life. The tradition is consistent in pointing out that he was a prince of Kanchi. His association with Tamil-speaking Kanchi is confirmed by the Japanese form of his name: Bodai-daruma, shortened to Daruma. The Tamil form is Bodi-daruma. The Japanese name Daruma goes back to an ancient popular name of the Master. Moreover, the tradition that the doctrine was transmitted from Mahakashyapa to Bodhidharma appears to have a basis. It seems that the modern Kacchapeshvara Temple at Kanchi was a Buddhist sanctum in ancient times, dedicated to Mahakashyapa, the first patriarch of Dhyana Buddhism. To this day there are some Buddhist sculptures in this temple. The tradition of the twenty-eight patriarchs of Dhyana Buddhism can thus be of Indian origin.

There are three basic scriptures of Zen: Lankavatara-sutra, or the Sutra of the Journey to Lanka (Ceylon); Vajracchedika Prajnaparamita, or the Diamond Sutra; and the Hymn to Nilakantha Lokeshvara, the hymn to the Blue-necked Lord.

Bodhidharma took Gunabhadra's translation of the Lankavatara-sutra as its scripture, as it was the only available Chinese version at the time.

The "Record of the Succession of the Dharma-treasure", a history of Zen Buddhism discovered from the Tun-huang Caves, says that the first patriarch of the Lankavatara as representing the Dharma-treasure was Bodhidharma who revealed the inner meaning of the Sutra. The connection of Bodhidharma and Lankavatara is thus intimate. Lankavatara can refer to the journey from Kanchi to Ceylon. It is stated in the life of Hsuan-tsang by Hui-li: "Kanchipura is the sea-port of South India for Ceylon, the voyage to which takes three days." Moreover, subtle nuances point to Kanchi as the native place of Bodhidharma and as the home of Zen. The tea ceremony ends with the banging of the lid on the teapot. When I enquired of my Japanese host, Prof. Chikyo Yamamoto, he said: "Master Bodhidharma used to slam the lid in times of yore." How Indian! I was sure once again: It must go back to Bodhidharma.

The Zen adepts reject the written word and claim an unwritten doctrine, transmitted from mind to mind, where the heart of man directly sees into its own nature. Yet, when Hui-neng was invested as the Sixth Patriarch, the corridor was painted with scenes from the Lankavatara, besides the paintings of the Five Patriarchs Transmitting the Robe of Bodhidharma and the Dharma as a testimony for future generations. Bodhidharma had sanctioned the lineage of five Chinese Patriarchs of Zen in a *gatha* that ran: "one flower with five petals is unfolded". In its earlier phases Zen Buddhists were mainly a kind of Lankavatara sect. The teachings of inner realisation of the Lankavatara provide a philosophical basis for the transcendental intuition of Zen. In the Lankavatara, Buddha tells Mahamati to attain a state of inner realisation (*pratyatmagocara*) and when one has inner knowledge one is enlightened. The

古寺天寒夜一宵不禁風冷雪飛々豌

吾豈與何寺特巴取堂中木佛燒

A monk burning a wooden statue. Finest handscroll by Indra in the 14th century.

Lankavatara is unique in emphasising that life is experiencing truth: seeing must be living, and living, seeing. The Lankavatara certifies the existence of the Buddha-mind in each one of us, and provides Zen its doctrinal base. The Lankavatara forbids meat-eating and recounts eight reasons for abstaining from meat. To take the lives of animals and eat their flesh is like eating our own. Eating meat is spiritual pollution. To this day, food in Zen monasteries is vegetarian. While Zen stands on its own, the Lankavatara confirms it and is also its philosophical essence.

The Lankavatara was highly philosophical and abstruse to the Chinese. During the time of the Sixth Patriarch Hui-neng, the emphasis shifted to the Vajracchedika, the Diamond Sutra, which was more understandable than the recondite Lankavatara. Besides meditation, painting was the other forte of Zen.

The Diamond Sutra, scripture of transcendental wisdom, lent itself admirably to the tenor of Zen painting. The Ch'an masters of Mid T'ang were distinguished by their non-conformist techniques of painting. Wang Mo "Ink Wang" painted landscapes starting from configurations of ink splashes, in the manner of Zen painters who delighted in expressing their sincerity in trans-logical forms like a "one-stroke" Bodhidharma, the Ippitsu

Daruma by Shokai Reiken (1315-1396). The dictum of the Vajracchedika Prajnaparamita, "Form is emptiness and emptiness is form", inspired Zen art which vanished into nowhere, with its diaphanous water colours and empty spaces interfering with the coherence of thought and form. A painting shimmered in meditation. Zen was deeply steeped in the Prajnaparamita philosophy of *Shunyata,* or emptiness.

A scroll of the Prajnaparamita is held in the hand of Manjushri, whose image can often be seen in the Meditation Halls (zendō) of Zen monasteries. Manjushri expounds only this book, the doctrine of *Shunyata* which has exerted a decisive influence on the thought of Zen.

As the Ideal Teacher and the Eternal Teacher, Manjushri is venerated by Zen Buddhists, to whom the teacher-disciple relationship is fundamental.

The Dharani to Nilakantha Lokesvara is what the Zen monk reads in his daily service. The eminent role of the Nilakantha hymn in Zen points to a milieu dominated by Buddhism and Shaivism in equal measure. Kanchi, the hometown of Bodhidharma, was a prominent seat of Shaivism, besides Buddhism and other denominations.

The practice of meditation in Japan goes back to Dosho, the founder of the Yogachara (Hosso) sect. He went to China in 653, and became a disciple of Hsuan-tsang, the great pilgrim. On his return, he constructed the first meditation hall within the first Hosso Monastery. Tao-hsuan was the first Chinese Zen monk to come to Japan. He taught Zen meditation to Gyokyo, the teacher of Saicho (767-822), the founder of the Tendai sect. Contemplative tradition became integral to Tendai.

It was in the 12th century that Eisai (1141-1215) pioneered the transmission of Rinzai sect, and Dogen (1200-1253) the Soto sect. In 1191 Eisai founded Shofukuji, the first Rinzai centre in Japan. In 1202 Kenninji was the first large-scale Zen monastery. Eisai was invited by the government to Kamakura. Here he constructed the Jufukuji monastery which was to become the greatest bastion of Zen. Henceforth Zen flourished at both the cultural cities of Kyoto and Kamakura and grew rapidly. Japanese monks journeyed to China to study at, and to perform pilgrimage to, the "Five Mountains and Ten Monasteries". Zen towered over Japanese culture, making notable contributions to popular and higher education, producing vigorous masters, expressive calligraphy, and painters with a tectonic monumentality.

Tradition records that the Buddha handed over Zen to Mahakashyapa. It passed on from him on to the twenty-eighth patriarch Bodhidharma, the first patriarch in the Chinese transmission. Yet the accent of Zen masters has been that its ultimate authority issues out of direct personal experience. In whatever situation a person be, he is always free in his inner life. Zen is "self-reliance" (*jiyu*) and "self-being" (*jizai*).

Riddles exude from the mind as clouds rise from mountain peaks. As Zen masters say, "examine the living words and not the dead ones". The mind awakens a consciousness attuned to the pulsation of Reality. The cosmic conscious is not revealed unless one experiences *samadhi (sammai),* a state of one-pointedness (*ekagrata*), again a link with the Lankavatara

The eternally serene *vivikta-dharma,* the spirit of Eternal Loneliness of the Lankavatara, is the *sabi* of Zen that conditions landscape gardening, tea-ceremony, flower-arrangement, furniture, and so on. It has elements of simplicity and naturalness, familiarity and refinement, commonness veiled with a mist of inwardness. The Zen sense of the Alone is represented in the "thrifty brush": a minimum of lines to express a plenitude of form. It is the aesthetic appreciation of absolute poverty, of austere form. The poetic form *haiku* is poverty (*hin*), is loneliness itself. Its foremost poet Basho was an incarnation of Eternal Loneliness:

A branch shorn of leaves
A crow perching on it—
This autumnal eve.

A raven on a dead branch of a tree: it is the great Beyond. Eternal Aloneness is *fuga*, "refinement of life". A pure, serene mind alone can enjoy the absolute aloneness. The environment has to be free from defilement: not a speck of dust in the thatched hut in the courtyard (*roji*) of the monastery, and there shines the mind undisturbed.

Zen is transcendental aloofness amidst things worldly, to feel the inward presence of the highest values. It is a longing for primal simplicity, to be in the bosom of nature to feel her pulsations. Draw bamboos for ten years, become a bamboo, then forget all about bamboos when you are drawing. This is the Zen of the bamboo: to become one with the spirit that is bamboo. Instincts and intuitions merge into *prajna*—immovable. As the primal poet Valmiki was so moved by a hunter shooting a love-lorn pair of birds that he spontaneously composed the *shloka* metre, likewise Zen monks view sparrows in a special light. The Zen artist Ten-am Kaigi likens two sparrows to the two disciples of Sakyamuni: Mahakashyapa and Maudgalyayana. The painting "Sparrows and Bamboo", attributed to Mu-ch'i (13th century), has been praised through the centuries. Affectionately termed "Wet Sparrows" the two birds are huddled together, dampened by a chill rain. It depicts the oneness of all Life, whether human or avian. The Rigveda speaks of the symbolism of two birds. In a touching tribute to his dead pet sparrow, Ikkyu dedicated a gatha in 1453, in which he likened its passing to the final nirvana of Sakyamuni. Zen masters saw a parellel between an enlightened individual and a sparrow uninhibited in its spontaneous joy: the *sat-chidananda* of Vedanta, the true bliss of the mind.

The Zen *haiku* is brevity and austere simplicity. It recalls the *sutra* style in Sanskrit where the decrease of half a vowel in a grammatical *sutra* was celebrated like the birth of a son. As with Indian poets, the cuckoo is favourite with Japanese poets. Once Chiyō (1730-75) the *haiku* poetess called on a noted *haiku* master. He gave her the conventional theme of the cuckoo:

Hearing a cuckoo cry,
I looked up in the direction
Whence the sound came:
What did I see?
Only the pale moon in the dawning sky.

The poetess made several attempts but the master rejected them as untrue to feeling. She pondered a whole night, and as she noticed the light of dawn trickling in, the following *haiku* formed in her mind.

Calling "cuckoo", "cuckoo",
All night long,
Dawn at last.

The thatched hut, the *parna-kuti* of India, has become the aestheticism of simplicity in the art of tea. It is austere in architecture, a proximity to roots, stripping off of all artificial trappings. The ritual of tea was introduced in Japan by the Zen master and National Teacher Dai-o in 1267. The tea ceremony comprises the feeling of harmony (*wa*), reverence (*kei*), purity (*sei*), and tranquillity (*jaku*).

These four elements constitute an orderly life in a Zen monastery. Tea-drinking is cultivating the inner field of consciousness. Sitting in a semi-dark and irregular room, a crudely formed tea bowl eloquent with the personality of the maker, listening to the sound of boiling water, the sound of water dripping from a bamboo trough outside the hut, induce a state of tranquillity (Sanskrit *samatha*). Tea is a psycho-sphere. Lord Krishna speaks of the flowers, leaves, fruits, and water as offerings to Him in the fullness of the heart. Toyotomi Hideyoshi, a patron of the art of tea, gave this verse to his master Sen no Rikyu (1521-91):

When tea is made with water drawn from the depths of Mind
Whose bottom is beyond measure,
We really have what is called cha-no-yu.

The Bhagavad Gita was revealed on the battlefield of Kurukshetra, In India sword and scripture (*sastra* and *sastra*) were one. So was Zen the spirit of the Samurai. It taught him to treat life and death as one, as non-duality, in Japanese, *mu-ni*, "not two". Zen is will-power urgently needed by the warrior. The Japanese say: *ken zen ichi* "the sword (*ken*) and Zen are one (*ichi*)". Sages like Drona from the epic Mahabharata are great masters of the art of war in the Indian tradition. The Zen masters too were famous teachers of swordsmanship. Zen gives a resolute mind. A Zen warrior hates to meet death lingeringly. He desires to be blown away like the cherries before the wind. Fearlessness (*abhaya*) in a fleeting world of non-reality. Avalokiteshvara (Kannon Bosatsu) is the 'giver of fearlessness' and all *haiku* poets worship Kannon and are hence fearless. The sword is identified with annihilation of things that lie in the way of peace, justice, and humanity. Sword is the embodiment of life and not of death. Manjushri carries a sword in his right hand and a *sutra* in his left. A Zen master knows when and how to wield each of them. A master of the sword or the spear is called *osho* in Japanese, which is *ojha* in Hindi and *upadhayaya* in Sanskrit, the title of a Buddhist priest. The hall in which swordsmanship is practised is termed *dojo*, the place of enlightenment, *bodhi-manda* in Sanskrit. Zen rids the swordsman's mind of the desire to play a passive role.

From the swordsmanship hall (*dojo*) to the garden. No gardens in the world are more abstract and symbolic than those inspired by Zen. A Zen garden is a starting point for meditation, a possible gate to *satori*, to delivery from the bondage of illusion and the chains of reincarnation. It is the mystery of autonomy and spontaneity. Every stone has its innuendo, every blade of grass touches off a vortex of reflections. The Ryoanji garden, with its naked expanse of white sand acting as a setting for stones takes us back to the sea, to the ocean of existence (*bhava-sagara*). This supremely abstract monument, the *kare sansui*, the "dry landscape" garden, was designed in the late fifteenth century. The rocks, tiny mounts Fuji, simply mean *fuji*, not two, that is peerless, the abolition of all distinctions, the *advaya*. There are both literal levels and symbolic tangents thereof, crossing the seas of illusion towards the shore of *satori*, "illumination", to cross over the dry sandy ripples of the ocean of existence, the *bhava-sagara*.

Zen is a product of the Chinese and Japanese soil from the Indian seed of Enlightenment, India's hut and Japanese bamboos, India's sophisticated thought and the bizarre koans: all leading to self-reliance (*jiyu*) and self-being (*jizai*).

Red-Robed Bodhidharma, by an unknown artist. Silk scroll with a colophon by Tao-lung (1231-1278).

Martial arts of India: Kalaripayattu

G. SANKARA PILLAI

Thang-Ta

E. NILAKANTA SINGH

India has a long and distinguished tradition of martial arts involving different physical disciplines. Some of these are described in ancient texts, which speak of the training and skills required in fields as diverse as archery, fencing, wrestling, spear fighting and unarmed combat. Mere physical prowess was not enough; it had to be accompanied by an austere discipline of the mind and sharpened reflexes. The body became an instrument of the mind; and attack and defence were carried out not by brute strength but through the alert and intelligent use of an agile and flexible body.

From the vast array of Indian martial arts, we will take a look at two: *Kalaripayattu* from Kerala and *Thang-Ta* from Manipur. At first glance, no two places could be more unlike. These two states of India, one located in the extreme south west of the country and the other in the north east, are at opposite ends of the sub-continent.

The deadly ballet of the martial arts : Thang-Ta, above, and Kalaripayattu, top right.

Coastal Kerala is washed by the waters of the Arabian Sea and has the lush green vegetation and palms of the tropics. Manipur is a valley ringed by mountains. Ethnically and in terms of language and culture, they illustrate the diversity that is India; yet the similarity of their strong traditions proves here, as elsewhere, the bond that unites the country.

Kalaripayattu

The cultural pattern which evolved in Kerala is unique to this state. *Kalaripayattu*, very often lauded as a major contribution of Kerala to world culture, is also one of the main forces that has influenced the development of Kerala's traditional theatre forms.

The word *Kalari* can be traced back through many centuries. Though there is no undisputed information available about its first usage, certain scholars trace it back to the myth of the sage Parasurama who is said to have created Kerala by flinging his axe into the sea. According to "Keralolpatti", the traditional chronicle of Kerala, Parasurama initiated 108 *Kalaris* and donated swords to 36000 Brahmins. The ballads of North Kerala, which sing of the brave exploits of heroes and heroines, very often refer to the *Kalari* system of training. Occasionally they give full details of the establishments of *Kalaris*, the rituals in connection with the commencement of training, and the various processes involved in the training schedule. M.D. Raghavan, in his treatise on folk plays and dances, states that the word *Kalari* has been derived from the Sanskrit term *Khalorika*, which stands for a military training ground. Unfortunately only a few books or manuscripts which deal with this particular and highly sophisticated physical training system are available to us today. We may note, however, that in its original usage, *Kalari* was the common name given to all places of learning, including primary education centres, and its meaning was not restricted to a centre for physical training.

Multiple forces were at work in giving shape to the practice of *Kalari*. There are various speculations among scholars about the origin of the system in Kerala. A few scholars believe that the spread of Brahminism influenced rise of the *Kalari* system. *Dhanurveda* is considered to be the scripture of all combat training systems and so this particular type of training must also have been carried out in the various learning institutions established by the Aryans when they came to this coastal strip of land. There are early references to certain *Shalas*, considered to be places of learning, such as Kanthalore *Shala*, Parthivapuram

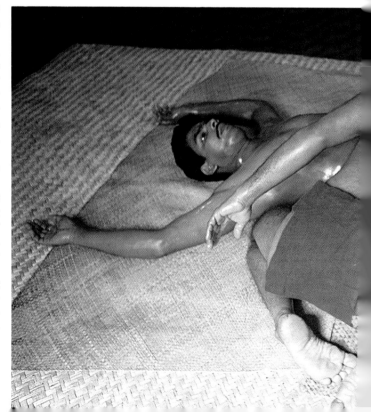

Opposite page : Kalari student salutes the teacher near the 'poothara' or shrine. Left : a student is massaged with medicinal oil. Above : Kalari combatants face each other with sword and spear.

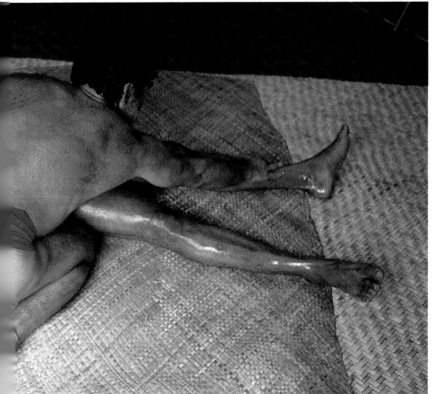

211

Shala, and so on. Some hold the view that these *Shalas* were the forerunners of the *Kalari*. Kerala history reveals the establishment of certain groups of trained soldiers who are equated with the suicide squads of the Middle Ages and whose important function was the protection of religious centres. We have evidence of combat training systems all over the west coast, even all over India. That such training systems were strongly established in the Middle Ages is clear from references in the travelogues of European visitors such as Barbosa, Capt. Neehalf and Johnston.

There is a strong claim that *Kalaripayattu* is the original source of Karate. Such a theory is supported by the argument that the system might have travelled to Japan through China along with the spread of Buddhism. Buddhist *Maths*, or religious establishments, might have accepted these training programmes. Moreover it is thought that the *Shalas* mentioned above were actually Buddhist institutions of learning. Additionally the interpretation of the word kara-te (empty hand) reminds us of the various patterns of bare-handed fight and defence included in the *Kalaripayattu* system, adding strength and credence to the argument.

But *Kalaripayattu* was not designed as a mere combat training system, even though it includes all modes of duels and the intricate use of weapons in offence and defence. Above all, *Kalaripayattu* aims at strengthening the body to transform itself to become the abode of a strong and powerful mind. This co-ordination of mind and body is vital to *Kalaripayattu*, and is explained in detail in every authentic text written on the subject. *Kalaripayattu* demands the fusion of mental and visual concentration with superb physical technique. Psycho-physical integration is essential, calling for a tightly controlled energy flow, and a highly responsive body.

This exacting system of training is capable of producing a combatant who can face any opponent on his own terms. Despite the potential deadliness of the variety of weapons used in *Kalaripayattu*, they are considered as no more than extensions of the human body. Long before he is instructed how to use weapons, the student must undergo extensive training to gain total control of his mind and body. The art of fencing, and the scientific handling of a sword, dagger or stick both in attack and defence attains a high degree of perfection in this system, and the status of the training is as important as that of academic learning. Traditionally *Kalaripayattu* was taught in the afternoons, after the normal school was over. Reading, writing and arithmetic in the mornings, and the handling of the sword, the spear and the stick in the afternoons, this was the rule.

The establishment of the *Kalari* was under a pattern of social order and religious environment. The traditional gymnasium or *thara* is described in detail in the books written on the subject. The simple building is oblong and slightly below ground level, with its gabled roof and four sides covered with plaited cadjan leaves. The length of the room runs to 42 feet on an east-west axis, though slight variations of dimension are possible. The entrance is always through a flight of steps from the eastern side. The spartan bareness of the room, with its floor of hard-packed earth, is broken by the *poothara* or seven-tiered shrine in the south western corner.

The number of deities enshrined in the *Kalari poothara* range in number from seven to twentyone, but the presiding divinity in all cases will be the Kalari Bharadevatha, identified as the goddess Bhadrakali. The *poothara* has several steps leading to a tiny raised platform, where there are offerings of flowers and *tulsi* leaves. The *Gurukkal* or teacher is revered as the representative of the deity and is considered the living embodiment of a long line of *Gurus*. He is entitled to the same reverence due to the Gods. Before stepping into the training ground every student reverently touches the floor with his right hand and places it ritualistically on his forehead as a form of salutation. He does his obeisance to the *poothara* and does *sarvanga namaskaram*—a salutation to the *guru* by prostrating himself at his feet.

A boy is enlisted as student on an auspicious day, usually at the age of seven, He gives an offering or *dakshina* to the *guru* and is then initiated into the process with the first lesson. Though the *Kalari* system with its elaborate process of training is designed for males, females are not completely barred from admission as is evident from the stories of *Kalari* queens described in ballads like 'Unniyarcha'. Females as a rule were trained not so much to be fighters but to attain good physical form and health.

There is an elaborate system of *uzhichil* or body massage which is done for a fortnight and is repeated every year. If at the time of initiation the student is young, *uzhichil* is done by hand, and if he joins at a more mature age the massage is done with the feet. There are various methods of doing this, and all methods are described in detail in ancient manuscripts such as "Maipayattu". The *vaitharee* or rhythmic vocal utterances rendered along with the physical work are also detailed in the books.

In the training of the body there are certain important actions like *kuttinirutuka* and *thudakku chavitti amarthuka*. These are all adopted with the view to give maximum flexibilty to the body.

The *uzhichil* is done to serve more than one purpose. The oil for the massage has therapeutic value as well, and is used for the treatment of physical ailments. This system basically aims at preparing the physique and the entire muscular system to cope with any challenging situation, for the *Kalari* massage is designed to give the body not only flexibility but also strength.

The total process of training can be divided into three distinctly different periods. The first phase is the period of Maipayattu. The important items are *nerkal, veethukal, irrutikal, thiruttukal* and *konekal*, a disciplined series of movements that exercise every part of the body to give ultimate control and agility. There are different variations of all these with different names. At the end of this phase, the student reaches a level of body control that enables him to leap, twist, jump and turn upwards, forwards and backwards in easy, fluid movements. During the second phase the trainee is taught various movements using a stick. Here the *payattu* or element of combat between two opponents begins, going on to using the *muchan*, a shorter stick, to gain greater expertise during this period. The third and last phase of training uses more intricate and dangerous weapons. After the student has attained mastery in the preliminary process he receives his fencing lessons. This begins with the *muchan* otherwise called *cheruvadi* or *kuruvadi;* a short stick one and a half inch in diameter and 18 to 24 inches in length.

C.V. Narayanan Nair, in 1933, said: "I started training in my fencing school Kerala Kalari by name, near the Mahadevar Temple at Thiruvangad in Tellichery six years ago. Here I gave regular instruction in the customary fencing exercises, that is; 1. Body control (*meyyivakkom*) 2. Twelve spanner (*kethi kayari*); 3. Three spanner (*cheruvadi*); 4. Dagger (*Otta*) 5. Spear (*Kalaripayattu*); 6. Sword play (*puliyamkom*)." *Otta* is described by him as a form of dagger curved like a scimitar and having a strong

Kalari teacher and his pupil in a thrilling duel with short-handled daggers.

guard for the fist. Manoeuvres with this weapon are dangerous and need perfect mastery and skill. In wielding this weapon all strokes are directed to the 64 *kulamarmam*-s or most vital parts of the body (from the fencer's point of view there are 107 *marmam*-s of the body of which 64 are *kulamarmam*-s). The secrets of successful swordmanship are however taught only to those disciples of the *guru* in whom he has perfect confidence. Many people who have either witnessed or come into contact with the daily practice of this art of fencing have praised it, pointing out the strength, flexibility and energy which it gives to physical accomplishments.

Thus this system of *Kalaripayattu*, though aimed at preparing eminent warriors, had the much loftier ideal of developing physical capabilities to such a point that the body became a pure and simple instrument upon which could be played the subtlest possible emotional notes to the wonderful rhythm of the music of the limbs and hands. No wonder, then, that this indigenous system of physical culture made a valuable contribution to the creation of rustic as well as sophisticated performing art forms.

It is against this background of the development and establishment of the *Kalaripayattu* system that we should note the performing art forms of Kerala and the influence of *Kalari* on them. Viewing the most important art forms of Kerala, such as Theyyam and Padayani, which are for the most part ritualistic, or more sophisticated dance and drama forms like Koodiyattom and Kathakali, we discover that the steps and hand gestures very much resemble those of the *Kalari* fighter and the training process for the physique. These performing art forms owe very much

to the *Kalaripayattu* training system. Their basic elements of steps, gestures, and postures are adopted from this great art of physical culture. The influence is clearly discernible in recently created art forms like Chavittu Natakam. The performing art of a more martial nature known as *velakali* clearly shows all the elements taken from this ancient physical training system. No performing art of any worth can be cited as an exception to this rule.

This famous system has, over the years, gone into a decline, though in recent times there has been an awakening of interest throughout Kerala. According to Ramavarma Appan Thampuran, a famous writer in Malayalam, the decline of the *Kalari* system started with the invasion of Tippu in the eighteenth century. But there might have been multiple reasons for this unfortunate state of affairs. The change of the socio-political establishment because of colonisation, the accompanying change in values, might have in some way given a severe blow to the *Kalari* system. That it was not exterminated completely proves the mighty hold it once had on society and daily life. The impact of such changes was two fold. Even when the values attached to the western model of life gained popular acceptance, a minority clung fanatically to the old traditions, and tried to keep the flame of this physical culture from complete extinction. Another more creative and indirect effect of the jolt was its gradual permeation into the various performing art forms of the state. Synthesised with other traditional inspirations, this ancient system helped in the evolution of highly sophisticated performing art forms.

There is an old saying in Malayalam which lays down

213

the rule that for skill in fencing exercises, the whole body must become an eye. In other words, the whole muscular structure must be made as sensitive, responsive and alert as the human eye. This is the fundamental principle on which the *Kalari* training system is designed.

Manipuri Thang-Ta

Manipur in north east India is an area where hills surround the valley at the centre. This central valley is the abode of the largest and the most advanced community of the state, known as the Manipuris or technically speaking, the Meiteis. The Meiteis belong to the Indo-Mongoloid group of people. Manipuri or the Meitei language belongs to the Tibeto-Burman group of languages (Kuki-Chin) whose origins are believed to be in south west China, from where waves of people came into India, some of them entering Assam along the Brahmaputra river and possibly Manipur also. The Manipuris of the valley have of course, been exposed to various cultural influences from all directions—east, north, south and west. The Aryan Brahmins started arriving from all parts of India from 15th century A. D. and merged with the local people. So also the Chinese, Burmese Shans and Tais, all of which led to a composite racial group known as the Meiteis. Manipur also belongs to the Tantric belt, right from Tibet and Bhutan and extending upto Assam and Bengal. The Hindu neo-Vaishnavite movement from 18th century A.D. gave a new dimension to Manipuri culture.

Manipuri culture presents a remarkable fusion of aesthetic and ethical aspects. The aesthetic culture comprises dance and music which is well known all over the world. Yet will, character and self-discipline constitute the first condition for human self-perfection. This constitutes the ethical dimension of Manipuri culture. *Tapas,* the energising conscious power of cosmic being, and *Ananda,* with its delight of self-creation and self-experience, blend harmoniously in Manipuri culture. *Thang-Ta* constitutes the core of the ethical culture of the Manipuris.

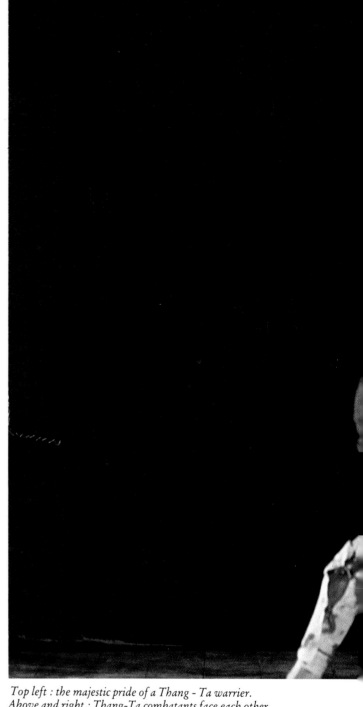

Top left : the majestic pride of a Thang - Ta warrier.
Above and right : Thang-Ta combatants face each other with a variety of weapons — sword, spear, shield.

214

The Meiteis are a martial race and throughout history have fought with honour and valour. Training in the martial arts was at one time obligatory for youth, who might be called upon to fight for their chieftain or king against the Burmese, the Chinese, the Khasis or the tribals of the surrounding hills. Thus the importance of *Thang-Ta* as an art for self defence and of course, for offence. But apart from its long historical tradition, *Thang-Ta* has a spiritual foundation, having its roots in Tantra.

The old gurus of *Thang-Ta* were deeply involved in the Tantric Sadhana or discipline of *Mantra* (incantation) and *Yantra,* and the utilisation of occult forces and extra sensory perceptions. Tantra is not merely Hindu, but it can be Buddhistic or may have its roots in the Indo-Mongoloid culture of pre-historic times. It has assumed many forms or levels of expression, but the basic statement of the concept of God, Nature and Man is that there is one Reality which cannot be described or defined; it is supreme, absolute. It is what is called *Parashiva*, the trans-

Top and above : female Thang-Ta contestant defeats her male rival. Opposite page : Thang-Ta warrior prepares to leap into combat.

cendent. That reality is self-existent. When this Reality has the mood to manifest, there is a vibration called *spanda*. It becomes Shiva and Shakti, the static consciousness and dynamic consciousness. The Tantra Yoga looks upon the human body as a miniature universe. Just as there is a divine consciousness in the universe, so there is the same consciousness in the human body also. But this consciousness is ruled by ignorance and falsehood. To recover true consciousness, Tantra provides many disciplines, chiefly three: (1) the Deity, the Godhead, (2) the form, either a *murti* or a diagram in the form of a circle or a triangle—"a *yantra* or a configuration of forces represented by the Deity", (3) *mantras*, certain words or syllables which constitute the "aural" emanation of the Deity.

According to an old tradition in Manipur, the use of a spear or a sword with certain steps is associated with the creation of the world. The Lord asked His eldest son to create the world and on the request of the son, opened His mouth and showed him the world of nerves inside. He asked His son to create the same pattern outside, which he did with the help of nine gods and seven goddesses who were created out of Him. This episode, allied to the Tantric world, links the microcosm to the macrocosm.

This resulted in the complex and esoteric movements of *Thengou*, based on the first steps of creation, sacred and ritualistic, executed by the dancer with a sword or spear on the symbolic head of a thousand-petalled lotus or a thousand-headed snake. The movements vary from vigorous to gentle, from stamps of the foot to careful treads, and the nine styles of *Thengou* are always accompanied by the incantation of *mantras*, the syllables which are the aural emanations of the Deity. But in the rituals of

Khousarol also has a legendary background but it is more virile and secular, the names being associated sometimes with particular hill tribes of Manipur. Every artist has to introduce himself and the principality (called Paana) to which he belongs, offering himself to the gods *Pakhangba* and *Sanamahi*. The sequence starts with a shout (which may be called *Salami*) and comprises stages of turns, jumps, steps, forward and backward twists. Performed before large audiences during festival times, each of the styles of the spear dances has a fixed sequence and calls for great skill and agility. The changing patterns of attack and defence are so swift that often the bodies are a blur of movement and the spear seens to have a life of its own. Each bout is fast-paced, with the performers leaping, bending and swaying, sometimes apart, and sometimes locked in combat. It is a happy sign that *Ta-Khousarol* is being revived with great enthusiasm with the help of the living *gurus* and warmly accepted by youth in their quest for identity.

The sword generally goes with the spear, and mastery of both arts was once required of every warrior or youth. As with the spear, the sword has its different types of shapes and even distinctive names. The expert swordsman carries, besides the *chungoi* or shield, three types of swords such as *yet-thang* (right hand sword) *oithang* (left hand sword) and *tendong-thang*, an additional sword kept on the back and used like an arrow in times of emergency. The art of sword fighting has most probably been influenced and enriched by similar arts of fencing from other parts of India. But it still preserves its distinctive character. The art of sword fighting has its particular steps and jumps; here again, swift graceful movements make it a thrilling spectacle. Among the variations in performance are fighters facing each other with swords in both hands, the use of four swords demanding high technical virtuosity and ambidexterity from the combatants. Another variation has one fighter pitted against two opponents, calling for almost simultaneous attack/defence techniques. There are also performances where the sword fights the spear, or an axe, each demonstrating heights of excellence and artistry. It is extremely difficult for a swordsman to master all the variations of sword fighting, but he can master about 30 or so, depending on the number of footsteps and movements.

It is now evident that the art of sword and spear movements is an austere art and demands extreme discipline and courage from the student who must be aware of its spiritual foundation. Young boys of about 10 or 11 are initiated with an oath before the *guru* or teacher to always defend the weak and try to bring justice to the community. The serious student must study intensively for at least three years, absorbing both theory and practice under the watchful eye of his teacher. The theory studies the evolution and development of Meitei *Thang-Ta*. The practical aspect involves vigorous exercise of hands, feet and body to ensure the suppleness and flexibility so essential to the art. Basic movements and steps, body postures and poses are repeated until mastery over these is achieved. This is the grammar of the choreographed movement, designed to produce the sharp reflexes needed during improvised combat.

There are no standard rules for the various stages of learning the art. But the following steps would provide a rough model for the study of the sword fight. The student must master the art of holding the sword and the shield, and various poses with them. He must mark the steps with intense concentration, and learn to execute movements with the steps. He must locate the 26 areas for

Thengou are believed to lie the seeds of not only prosperity but also war, famine and destruction, the latter invoked if the performer makes a mistake. Thus *Thengou* has always been a secret art, revealed by its great masters only to a select few, and today it is almost dying out, hardly ever demonstrated.

Thang-Ta literally means "sword and spear" and these are the main weapons used. They are not, however, the only weapons, as the tradition of martial arts extends to the use of shields, sticks, axes and daggers. Within the generic term of *Thang-Ta* exist several forms, including *Thengou*; but what most spectators now see are variations of *Ta Khousarol*, the art of the spear dance, and *Thanghairal*, the art of sword fight. Mastery over both arts was a must for every warrior worth the name in Manipur.

As already mentioned, the history of Manipur is filled with fights and battles. It was only in the year 1891, when the Manipuris fought the last battle of independence and lost their freedom at the hands of British imperialism, that this art of *Thang-Ta* was suppressed in a systematic attempt to deprive the people of their heritage of martial arts. But fighting for honour and justice is deeply embedded in their blood. An old account of fights *(Chainarol)* in the Manipuri language gives remarkable examples of combat as a part of life yet imbued with a deep sense of courtesy. When an unarmed man was challenged, he could fetch his arms and fix a date for the contest. In spear bouts, the two rivals would measure out a distance acceptable to both, and standing or sometimes half-buried in the earth, would hurl spears at each other. It was a point of honour to surrender the first choice. A slight scratch on the body was sufficient to acknowledge defeat, and the vanquished would nobly accept death. Such was the code of honour in those times that sometimes the victor and the loser would share a good meal before the latter died. Their motto was: man has to submit himself both to God's law, which is inexorable, and the law of man against which it is possible to appeal. In case of enmity between two persons, both would normally agree to enter into a bout as an ordeal of God. Treachery on either side would be positively avenged at any cost, as God's law cannot be violated.

Ta Khousarol is the art of spear dance. The spear is of many types, and in olden days was used for specific purposes—to guard the king, to fight an elephant, or hunt a tiger. It is likely that the nine forms of *Ta Khousarol*, all of which are named, derive partly from the traditions of the hill tribes, and partly from those of the great masters.

Great concentration and discipline are required for the arts of Thang-Ta, leading to swift, exciting and always graceful movements.

strike in the human body, followed by practise of fights against the opponent.

It has now been increasingly proved that the steps, gaits and poses of sword and spear have contributed to the frame-work of some of the traditional dances of Manipur, such as the Lai-Haraoba, Raas Leela and Nata Sankirtana. The *Maibis* (priestesses) of Lai Haraoba have to execute a few graceful steps holding two swords in the hands. The *Chakra-hastas* or movements of both hands, a must for sword fight, are used in Lai Haraoba and Raas dances. The various poses and moves of Pala Cholom and Pung Cholom of Nata Sankirtana show certain basic movements of the art of sword and spear. The ethical culture thus provides the necessary background for the artistic expressions of the people.

This ancient art has been reborn, so to say, mostly in the form of decorative pieces or exciting composed fights. It is difficult to say if the swordsman and the spearman have been able to develop the sixth sense ("seeing through the ears and listening through the eyes"—as Paul Valery

used to say in a different context) associated with this aspect of Manipuri culture. But the way the artistes perform on the modern stage clearly indicates that this is not just a performing art. The arts of *Thang-Ta* are serious forms of self-defence, even aggression, now choreographed into swift, exciting and always graceful movements on the modern stage. Immense skill, agility and physical and mental discipline go into these performances. The seriousness with which these "fights" are presented clearly indicates that this is not just a dance form for enjoyment, but a study of movements full of surprise and dazzlingly executed leaps and thrusts. There is considerable room for improvisation, and so no two presentations are alike—unlike the codified movements of dance—maintaining excitement in each performance. The risks are enormous, as one false move could result in great injury. It is therefore the artistry of the performer, his high level of training, his anticipation of movements, that makes the Manipuri martial arts—known collectively as *Thang-Ta* —such a vivid and awesome spectacle. Beyond the training and its discipline lie the skill and artistry of the individual performers. To watch them in their deadly ballet, leaping, thrusting, tumbling, grappling, is to witness expressions of the body's power and beauty.

Towards tomorrow

DR. RAJA RAMANNA

The achievements of the century, which we are leaving behind in about the time of a decade, can only be termed as amazing in the history of mankind. Never before has the human race witnessed so many outstanding events in such a short period of time. It would have been a great credit to human creativity, had these great events led solely to the benefit of mankind. Unfortunately this has not been the case and the very stability of our society is still very much in question.

In predicting the future of our civilisation, it is necessary to review and assess some of the achievements of the past hundred years which can, without much controversy, be considered as epoch making. Without any doubt, the achievements of mankind in recent times have been in the field of science and technology. It has changed the world and has made man feel that he is supreme on this planet and quite possibly the whole of the solar system. Such unidirectional successes have made people believe that science controls the key to all progress, and that all other aspects of human civilisation are more or less obsolete and belong to museums.

Is this attitude justified? What position will the arts and philosophy take in a highly science-dominated world and can this domination last for ever? Is it possible that an over concentration on science and, particularly, technology can lead to a boredom that, in a fit of desire to be free from it all, man may rush towards solutions that could lead the world to an unprecedented disaster?

Even in this very century, although there are many things of which we can be very proud, disaster has always been round the corner. The two world wars of quite recent years, the attitudes of those in power, the complexes and conflicts of various ethnic and racial groups are obvious examples. Above all, jealousy, inherent in man, never seems to show a declining trend. One is unable to sit back and enjoy the peace of the rationality, if such a thing exists. In other words, the fundamental question of the next century is "Will man be able to overcome his suicidal instincts within the framework of a scientific philosophy and curb the excesses of a purely technological culture?" "Is the young science of psychology powerful enough in the face of abnormal conditions to rectify human behaviour collectively and individually?" The dividing line between normal and abnormal states in human behaviour is far from clear and it is quite possible that the part of our behaviour now classified as abnormal may, in fact, be the one responsible for its creativity.

If one is asked what have been the great achievements of man in this century, particularly in science and technology, one could make the following list in some

Man : caught in the contradiction between science and philosophy.

random order: The discovery of x-rays and radioactivity, the development of quantum mechanics, the discovery of nuclear fission, the understanding of the solid state of matter and its application to chemistry and metallurgy, the molecular understanding of biological structures, the agricultural revolution, discovery of antibiotics and the conquest of space.

In selecting these, there is no doubt that many very important items have been left out, but the ones which have been selected have had a strong social impact, besides possessing intellectual appeal. The discoveries have also brought with them a new set of problems of frightening quality.

The medical, agricultural and industrial uses of x-rays and radioactivity involve hazards that can result from misuse. Quantum mechanics has solved a great many scientific problems, but its foundations stress the need for a consistent philosophy of nature and seem to indicate the recognition of a consciousness existing separately of physics. It and the Godel theorem in Mathematics show that these theories by themselves question the absolute nature of truth in the sciences. Antibiotics have helped to overcome many dreadful killer diseases of the past but these have been replaced by new diseases for which cures are becoming more and more difficult. Besides, new drugs have side effects which seem more dangerous than the original disease. Nuclear fission, in spite of being the most important source of energy, has introduced large scale terror in the world, the magnitude of which could never have been imagined before and, now in conjunction with new materials, poses the greatest problem of survival. Under these circumstances, it is but natural to ask which way the world will turn in the years to come.

The progress of science and technology will continue as before, and the problems of Cosmology, the mysteries of the inner atom and the possibilities of the complex interactions within the solid state of matter will continue to occupy the interests of scientists for quite some time. There will be tremendous activity in these fields based on the achievements and resources created during this century. Old and awe-inspiring questions such as, whether there is extra-terrestrial life and whether there was a 'big bang' at all and, if so, what was science all about even before the bang, may find some answers. Biologists will continue to believe that they have the key to the understanding of what is 'life' and what causes consciousness on the basis of molecular biology, but the physicist (who is the closest to a philosopher among scientists) will continue to ques-

tion their claims. The controversies will always be there not because there will be a dearth of scientific facts; on the contrary, there will be plethora of them, what with robots, fast high-powered computers and large groups of trained people to interpret the data, but because of the inherent limitations of man himself. It is in his efforts to understand the nature of consciousness that man may find his defeat in his spirit of enquiry.

To find an integrated approach to knowledge, man has to depend, in the last instance, on his own brain. This living black box may be probed into for its detailed structure by all the power that science can provide, but the final appreciation of that very information will still have to be carried out by the brain itself. Such a situation will always allow for the type of paradoxes that Godel's theorem implies. Even the paradoxes of quantum mechanics belong to this class and, however much one tries to get away with statements like "Nature is like that, do not ask too many questions", it leaves one with an unpleasant and incomplete feeling. We will find ourselves in a situation when we cannot go on asking questions about ourselves without reaching a stage when the answers begin to beg the questions. We will have reached some sort of a condition of saturation. It is at this stage that one begins to feel the need of a philosophy to be able to live with the inconsistencies and the incompleteness of our systems within that framework.

Would the 20th century be able to give prescriptions on how the appreciative capacity of the mind can be enlarged? There is no doubt that drugs and chemicals affect the brain but could it ever be made to reach a super-conscious state? Certain temporary activity can definitely be enhanced by chemicals, but it seems to be only at the expense of its "normal" behaviour. The present state of knowledge would suggest that saturation in understanding cannot be broken by chemical interference.

The ancients had some prescriptions for widening the appreciation of thought processes. The countries of the East like Japan, India and China have much experience in these matters, though what has come down to us may not be reliable and is mixed with irrelevant material.

If we have to come to the conclusion that there are things for which we will never get to know the true answers within the present postulate of science, is it possible that the science of the 21st century will change the fundamental structure of the thinking processes of man? It is perhaps that, at this stage, the knowledge that we have relegated to the museums may come back to significance. Sometimes one has to look backward to move forward.